The Liturgy as Dance
and the Liturgical Dancer

CAROLYN DEITERING

THE LITURGY AS DANCE

and the Liturgical Dancer

✄ ✄ ✄

CROSSROAD · NEW YORK

1984
The Crossroad Publishing Company
370 Lexington Avenue, New York, N. Y. 10017

Library of Congress Cataloging in Publication Data
Deitering, Carolyn.
The liturgy as dance and the liturgical dancer.
Bibliography: p.143
1. Dancing — Religious aspects — Christianity.
2. Liturgics.   3. Religious dance, Modern.
4. Gesture in worship.   I. Title.
BV178.D35   1984   246.'7   84-12067
ISBN O-8245-0654-5 (pbk.)

To the Rev. Angelo Mastria, O. Carm., whose clear and loving celebration of The Dance first drew me into it,

and to my husband, Joe, who has supported and loved me throughout the writing of these pages.

Contents

Preface

I t is with no small amount of trembling that I title this book as I do. There is a danger. It may appear to be something it is not: a plea for "dancing at Mass." But while considering other titles, I keep coming back to this one because it alone finally says what the book is: a plea for beauty, integrity, and artistry in Christian worship.

The book *is* about movement, the art of movement. It is about that art which is the integrated and grace-filled action of the priest moving in accord with the rubrics indicated in the Sacramentary; the prayer-filled ritual gesture of members of the assembly; and the ministry of the trained liturgical dance artist offering an original work as a thread in the fabric of the liturgical dance par excellence, the liturgy itself.

It is also with no small amount of trembling that I attempt to define the liturgy as a dance, and to define the movement artist's role within that dance as one of transparent servant. Many good Christian people may wonder if the liturgy should be so moving as to tempt the word dance as descriptive of it. Many priests who move with clarity and beauty as they celebrate the liturgy may wonder at the suggestion that they are dancing. And many Christian dancers, formed by a secular world which places a premium on show and stardom may wonder at a definition of their art that calls them to a role of transparent servant. Yet that is the vision I would like to present, a vision formed by several decades of prayer and work in the fields of liturgy and dance.

The Liturgy as Dance and the Liturgical Dancer is offered

in the spirit of St. John the Baptist, and under his patronage. It is John the Baptist whose beginning was signaled by a sacred leap for joy in Elizabeth's womb, and whose ending was associated with a dance of quite another kind. It is his witness, in the third chapter of the gospel of John, which supports the vision of this book and challenges the art which it embraces:

"I must decrease, while he must increase."

The Dance

A s a child, I thought of and experienced God in terms of movement. God was the One who opened my eyes to the movement of the birch leaves flipping from green side to silver side on the tree in the front yard. He was the One who opened my ears to the roar of rolling waves off the New England coast where I sat while my grandfather painted his canvases, the One who opened my sense of touch to the warm breeze that danced over my face and limbs while I took a summer afternoon nap next to an open window. It was God who moved inside me when I pushed my scooter as fast as I could along the sidewalk, went as high as I could on the swing in the backyard, danced alone in the living room or outside in the rain, and took classes in the little dance studio in upstate New York. And it was God who was evident in the absolute stillness of things late at night after a snowfall. In church, I sat for what seemed like very long times and listened to what seemed like too many words. Occasionally I stood to sing, but other than that sat and listened. I wondered why the worship of God who made all things, including myself, to dance and roll and bend and flip didn't include some movement. But I loved God, and I knew the church was God's house, so if just sitting and listening was proper to God's house, that was all right with me.

When I grew older, I went to a university and studied about God. And everything I read about him reinforced my knowledge that he was a God of movement! In the beginning, God's Spirit moved over the face of the earth, causing everything to be in motion. Throughout the Old Testament, God invited his people to worship him in movement, to clap and shout, to lift up holy hands in prayer, to go in processions to the temple, to leap for joy, to rise and turn and walk and run, to dance. I learned that God, in the course of history and out of love for those he had created, became himself a human person, breathing and moving, naturally and freely. I learned that followers of Jesus, in the first five centuries of Christianity, exhorted believers to dance for the glory of God that dance which "uplifts every living body" and is "an ally of faith and an honoring of grace."[1]

When I left the university, I discovered among Christian churches a place where a great liturgical dance seemed to be going on every time people gathered for worship. Priest and people worshiped while bowing, genuflecting, prostrating, lifting up the precious elements, walking in procession, signing their bodies with the sign of Christ's redeeming cross, and at times kneeling breathlessly still. It seemed right that I find my way into this sacred dance, and after suitable preparation I did exactly that.

Fifteen years have passed since then, and in that time the Church has changed and grown, and so have I. Scholars and liturgists have begun to reveal the liturgy in its distilled essence and primary forms. Accumulated layers of repetitive or merely decorative practice have been swept away. As a dance artist working within this liturgical environment, I have been continuously challenged to discover and present in my art only that which is the distilled essence and primary form of things. It is an exciting time to be a Church artist.

One thing concerns me, however. It seems that as we have gathered more knowledge *about* the liturgy, we have been tempted to let go of some of our nonrational experiences *of* the liturgy. Because we are aware that we may have erred in the past by not thinking enough about what we were doing and why we were doing it, we now seem afraid of anything that cannot be intellectually grasped, or explained. "Full, conscious and active participation"[2] is encouraged, but it is usually limited to verbal and aural participation. Article 30 of the *Constitution on the Sacred Liturgy*, which says "the people should be encouraged to take part by means of acclamations, responses, psalms, antiphons, hymns, *as well as by actions, gestures and bodily attitudes*" (emphasis mine) is only half obeyed. Singing is "in"; profound bows are "out." The assembly is exhorted to sing and speak with force and volume, but no one seems to care if the sign of the cross is made with clarity. Although the Church in many places is opening itself to the possibility of dance as a viable liturgical art, it is in danger of losing The Dance!

The Liturgy as Dance and the Liturgical Dancer is offered for the sake of The Dance. It is offered for priests and ministers who seek to develop a language of celebrational movement which engages and unites the people assembled before them.[3] It is offered for members of the assembly, that they may embrace their "common gestures, movements and postures" of prayer with "an uncommon sensitivity."[4] And it is offered for Christian dance artists who strive to create "truly competent" artistry which glorifies God and "benefits the total liturgical action."[5]

It seems only fair that I introduce myself to the reader. I am, first, a lover of the liturgy, the source and summit of the Christian life[6] and the most profoundly incarnational of Christian arts. I am also a liturgical dancer, an artist who shapes movement—like a sculptor shapes clay, or a musician tones —into outward and sensible forms expressive of the inward and invisible realities of God received in word, sacraments, and the daily grind of life. I have worked as a full-time parish liturgist, responsible for all the words, sights, sounds, smells, tastes, and movements not specifically prescribed by rubric, and am keenly aware of the Church's desire for the "full, conscious and active participation" of the whole people of God, and the whole of each person, in the worship experience. I know that movement, the most basic language of expression and communication available to human beings, a language which all persons speak from before birth until the moment of death, has the power to integrate the whole person in the activity of liturgical prayer.

It is this language of movement, united with speech and song, which creates, in the words of Evelyn Underhill, the "art-form which is the vehicle of [the Church's] self-offering to God and communion with God."[7] It is this offering of movement and sound, of word and action, which is herein referred to as no less than The Dance.

❧ 2 ❧

Ritual and Creative Beauty

Worship is a fine art. As in any art, love is involved, and so is discipline. Is it not because of this polarity that we call quality life the art of living, quality love the art of loving, quality prayer the art of praying, quality anything the art of that anything?[1]

To call liturgical worship an art is not to say it is an action of human beings rather than of God. It is also not to say that ministers and worshipers are concerned with the outer appearances of their prayer rather than with the prayer itself or with God. There is no question of one *or* the other, of outer form or inner reality, of the action of God or the action of the Christian individual or community. An understanding of the nature of sacraments as outward and visible signs of inward and invisible realities precludes the need to separate the sensible from that which is beyond the senses. Faith in the Incarnation, the human appearance and reality of God, must lead to a deeply human involvement in the worship of God. An understanding of liturgy as the work of the people of God in cooperation with God's action requires that the community at worship does cooperate, and cooperate with every power of mind, body, and spirit which God has given. Good liturgy, and good art, are both divine *and* human. And liturgy must be art since it demands the best work, and all the love and discipline, which can be offered.

To call the liturgy *dance* is to raise it to the level of the highest of Christian arts. Dance, as it will be defined in this book, is the art of ritual and creative movement, the sole art which by its very being claims the power to unify body, mind, spirit, and emotions. Needless to say, a world of secular dance which emphasizes the body alone rather than the integrity of the whole person, which glorifies the body rather than rejoicing in embodiment, relinquishes its claim to be a true Christian art.

A few more definitions may prove helpful. *Beautiful* is a word often coupled with the word dance, but it is frequently used to refer to ways of moving which are not natural. "She moves like a rubber doll" or "he moves like an angel when he says Mass" are questionable ways to compliment the dance of creatures of flesh and blood. The movement of celebrant, assembly, or dancer is most beautiful when most natural, when most in accord with the God-given temperament and body structure of the person moving. It is beautiful when there is a deep correlation between the person moving, the movement being made, and the feeling being expressed.

Graceful is a troublesome word. Let us change that word to grace-filled and claim it as our own.

Artist: Ananda Coomaraswamy has said, "It is not that the artist is a special kind of person, but that each person is a special kind of artist."[2] Very scriptural. Each of us, made in the image of God, shares in God's creative life. Different persons are called to different intensities of artistic work, but all persons are creative. Our society tells us otherwise. When we were children we knew, in that way of knowing what we do not cognitively know, that we were creative, that we were artists. Now, when we are old enough to read this book, we believe otherwise. Statistics show that although 90 percent of 5-year-olds measure "high creativity," only 2 percent of adults measure the same. It is not that we lose what we had as children. Rather, it is drummed out of us by "the dirty devices of this world."[3]

What about the word *dancer?* Every human being who speaks the language of movement beautifully (meaning naturally), and accepts his or her grace-filledness and creativity is a dancer. We could reword Coomaraswamy's statement to say, "It is not that the dancer is a special kind of person, but that every person is a special kind of dancer." Again, different persons are called to different intensities of work in the art of movement. But there are none among Christian worshipers who should be labeled "nondancers." To label persons as such is to tell them they are incapable of giving beautiful and meaningful shape, in gesture and movement, to the invisible movement of the Spirit within. It is to deny them their Christian birthright and call to engage their whole being in The Dance.

Two final words require definitive attention: *ritual* and *creative.* Are they not incompatible opposites? Is it possible that the ritual movement of the priest-celebrant and assembly and the creative movement of the artist share a common ground? Can there be creativity in ritual movement, ritual in creative work?

Ritual movement is part of a highly symbolic system expressive of the faith of a community, and is manifest in oft-repeated and long-familiar forms which are heavy with meaning for that community. But true ritual is *living* ritual, containing the past, embracing the present, and allowing the future to unfold. Ritual which does not grow, naturally and organically, with the faith of the people who practice it, loses its claim to be ritual. It become ritualism. Meaningful form gives way to formalism. In a community as large and long-standing as the Catholic Church, organic change and creative development in ritual movement may proceed at what appears to be a ponderously slow pace. But therein lies a peculiar beauty. And there is challenge in patiently trusting the process, gently nudging it when necessary, but giving in neither to hasty change for the sake of change nor to a dull repetition of forms one despairs will ever change.

True *creative* movement "is the only, totally opposite, equivalent to ritual,"[4] and shares deeply in the nature of living ritual. The word creative is used often and unwisely to signify that which is innovative but unrooted, impulsive, without history. True creative movement, although continuously new, is rooted in its own history. It is organic, form growing out of form, formed by the meaning that needs to be expressed.

Ritual movement shapes, nourishes, and expresses the faith of a people. Creative movement digs down to express a particular depth of that faith or forges ahead to stand at the brink of faith. But both must be alive, both must grow organically, both must be deeply incarnational and committed to the embodiment of the Unseen.

❧ 3 ❧

Gift and Burden

I f we hope to open ourselves to a Christian art of movement and to the liturgy as The Dance, we must come to terms with the instrument of expression in dance, the body, and with the material of expression, bodily movement.

In the beginning, God created the human person a miracle of wholeness and integrity, embodied spirit, enspirited flesh. Throughout history, whenever God spoke to those he had created, he spoke not only to their minds, hearts, and imaginations, but also to their physical senses: through a burning bush, a voice, bare feet on holy ground, manna in the desert. And over and over again, God spoke to the human being through the sense of movement: come here, go there, bow down in worship, lift holy hands in praise, join in procession, shout, clap, dance!

In the course of history, God spoke intimately with his people by becoming himself a human person, Spirit Incarnate, one whose physical as well as spiritual senses were fully alive to the wonders of the Father. In declaring their witness to Jesus, the apostles rejoiced in the claim that their ears had heard, their eyes had seen, and their hands had touched the Word of life! (1 John 1:1). On the cross, Jesus saved the whole of the person the Father had created. Jesus did not die only for some spiritual "part" of the human person, for a soul imprisoned in an accidental body. Rather, he died, and rose, to save the whole of what the Father had created: body, mind, spirit, and emotions. He embraced and sanctified the human person "to the last shred and fibre" of his or her being.[1]

It is not surprising that the Christian Church has a long history of involving the whole person in worship. The sense of sight has been engaged by design, vestment, stained glass, and architecture; the sense of hearing by music and the spoken word; the sense of smell by the sweet odors of incense and flowers; the sense of touch by sprinklings with blessed water, anointings with oil, and the laying on of hands. The sense of taste has been engaged in the Lord's gift of himself in Bread to eat and Wine to drink. And the sense of movement — the kinesthetic sense — has been engaged in the actions, gestures, and bodily attitudes of celebrant, ministers, and members of the assembly.

Recent centuries have witnessed an increasing disregard for the whole person at worship, due both to our Western culture's exaltation of human intellectual powers and to forces within the Church which divided the human person into spiritual and intellectual "parts," considered to be good, and physical and emotional "parts," considered to be bad. Church documents written since Vatican II, however, reflect a renewal of concern for the integrity of the human person. "The liturgical celebrations of the faith community [Church] involve the whole person. They are not . . . merely rational or intellectual exercises, but also human experiences calling on all human faculties: body, mind, senses, imagination, emotions, memory. Attention to these is one of the urgent needs of contemporary liturgical renewal."[2] "Valid tradition reflects . . . attention to the whole person. . . . It is critically important . . . to reemphasize a more total approach to the human person by opening up and developing the nonrational elements of liturgical celebrations: the concerns for feelings of conversion, support, joy, repentance, trust, love, memory, movement, gesture, wonder."³ Human wholeness is a sacred gift. Reclaiming that gift, wherever it has been lost, is imperative for a Church that teaches that God has become a human person.

A vital point of reentry into wholeness and reclamation of the gift is the acceptance of bodily movement as a revelation of the inner life of the spirit and as a powerful shaper of that inner life. Because the human being is a unity of body, mind, spirit, and emotions, inner feeling is *expressed* outwardly in bodily movement (even when the resulting movement is a distortion of the inner reality), and bodily movement *impresses* its meaning and content on the inner self (whether or not the self invites it to do so). Within the liturgical setting, bodily movement can express feelings of adoration, praise, repentance, and joy, and it can help to form these attitudes when they are absent or only reluctantly present. The American bishops make a statement about music that can also apply to movement expression. "Faith does not always permeate our feelings. But the signs or symbols of worship can give bodily expression to faith as we celebrate. Our own faith is stimulated.... We rise above our own feelings to respond to God in prayer."⁴ When I want to be isolated and alone at Mass but must open myself to enfold the presence of God in another person at the Greeting of Peace, my antisocial feeling may flee no matter how hard I try to hang on to it.

Bodily movement is the most primary language of expression and communication available to us as human beings, a language we speak from before we are born until the moment of death, a language we speak all of the time whether consciously or unconsciously, On the most basic level, movement is the very sign of life. The sense of movement is a necessity for life. We could lose our other senses and still live. The loss of our sense of movement would spell quick disaster.⁵

From what we know about movement, the implications for liturgical prayer are enormous. Because movement is the sign of life, at once a necessity for life and the most primary language of human expression and communication, it is a powerful material to be tapped and shaped into prayer. The fact that we are saved as whole and integrated persons necessitates our acknowledging and celebrating that reality in the single language which manifests that reality. The fact that bodily movement has the power to both express and impress meaning makes it the most logical (for those who wish to be logical) and awesome (for those who wish to touch Incarnation, which is not logical) language of prayer and celebration available to the Christian Church.

Scripture tells us that the body is a temple of the Holy Spirit, that we are to glorify God in our bodies (1 Cor 6:19-20), that we are to offer our bodies in living sacrifice, holy and acceptable to God (Rom 12:1). But we have separated body and spirit. Inside the Church, we have allowed ourselves to think that if there is inner intention, the outer shaping of that intention is of no importance. Outside the Church, we have often found a world of movement expression and dance which places attention on the outer form alone, with no concern that the form be connected to any inner reality. Both our "religious" and our "worldly" views of bodily movement have missed the mark. One shuns the body. The other glorifies the body. Neither celebrates *embodiment*. Neither accepts the gift!

If some passages of Scripture seem to invite bodily movement in prayer, others might seem to discourage it. St. Paul's frequent opposition of the words body, flesh, and spirit might indicate that the body is of no import, or of negative import, in Christian life and worship. However, Paul does not tell the Galatians to crucify the body, but to crucify the flesh with its passions and lusts (Gal 5:24). Close exegetical study of the epistles reveals that "for Paul, 'flesh' is by no means equivalent to the body, and 'spirit' is by no means restricted to the soul.... 'Flesh' in the epistles denotes the *whole* man *qua* fallen, while 'spirit' denotes the *whole* man *qua* redeemed: the soul, therefore, as well as the body can become fleshly and carnal, and the body as well as the soul can become spiritual."[6]

When we fail to observe Paul's distinction between body and flesh, we fall into a Platonic dualism which sees the body as enemy rather than gift. Gerardus van der Leeuw, in his book *Sacred and Profane Beauty: The Holy in Art*, makes the point clear.

> True Christianity knows that body and soul were both equally created by God, equally attacked by corruption, and equally saved by Christ.... Genuine Christianity is in no sense dualistic. Therefore the idea that the movement of the body could express the holy is equally as right or wrong from a Christian point of view as the idea that the holy may be expressed through speech. Equally wrong, because nothing in this world is able to express the holiness of God; equally right because a duty has been given to man to glorify God with all his powers. Equally wrong because corruption resides in every human expression; equally right because man is created in the image of God.[7]

Even in eschatological theology, true Christianity knows no antagonism between body and spirit. "In the resurrection of the Lord, all things are made new. Wholeness and healthiness are restored."[8] The resurrection of the body, along with that of all creation, is promised. Although that promise is assuredly mysterious, we do confess that the human body is in God's scheme of salvation. We can say, along with St. Gregory Palamas, "If in the age to come the body will share with the soul in unspeakable blessings, it must certainly share in them, so far as possible, even now."[9]

Human limitations do confront us. Our daily striving to claim and reclaim God's gift of wholeness is only too real. But none of that excuses us from summoning every power, sense, and faculty to serve and worship the Father in our daily lives and in our liturgical prayer.

❧ 4 ❧

Sacred Act and Priestly Office

I n the history of ritual gesture and dance, there is much that predates the practices of Christianity to which this volume must necessarily be limited. A bibliography at the end of the book will guide the reader to sources of historical information about religious gesture and dance throughout the world.

A few preliminary comments, however, will lay a foundation for a treatment of dance in the Christian tradition. In the history of primitive societies, nothing approaches the dance in importance. Worship, work, play, the growing or killing of food, the fighting of spiritual or political battles, birth, puberty, marriage, and death, all are accompanied by dance, and in fact require dance. The unity of life, and the sacramental nature of life, demand that the individual or tribe enter into the movement (i.e., the life) of that from which it seeks power or seeks to empower or overpower. The dance is "no art that disregards bread; on the contrary, it provides bread and everything else that is needed to sustain life. It is not a sin, proscribed by the priest or at best merely accepted by him, but rather a sacred act and priestly office; not a pastime . . . but a very serious activity of the entire tribe."[1]

It would be a mistake to presume that primitive dancing is a phenomenon only of the past, since today there exist communities of persons who experience life as a whole and who express that wholeness in the most *primary* language available

15

to them. Of those communities, this author can speak first-hand of two; the Southwestern Indian and the Hawaiian Buddhist. The southwestern desert where I live is also home to the Yaqui and Papago Indian tribes. Although threatened by the encroachment of a segmented culture upon their way of life, both the Yaquis and the Papagos strive to continue their traditions of dance. Dances are performed yearly during Holy Week, on saint's days, and at Pow Wows. Attending a recent All-Indian Pow Wow, I was privileged to observe, and hear commentary on, several traditional dances. The spokesman for the Matachines explained that their dance, dedicated to the Virgin Mary, was "so holy" that it was rarely performed except in church. Another dance was introduced as one performed by men returning from war, its purpose being to restore the dancers to wholeness, to shake off evil and allow that evil to be returned to the earth to be purified. That day at the Pow Wow, the dance was performed by men who had served the United States in World War II and in Vietnam.

This year, at the 200th anniversary of San Xavier Mission just outside Tucson, the barriers which usually separate the Indian dancers from visitors were removed, and all were invited to join in the dance. At a recent Religious Education Congress workshop in Tucson, Mr. Rex Redhouse, a Navajo, taught several social dances, inviting all present to join. In concentric circles, holding hands, we learned a sideward stepping movement which we repeated over and over again to the accompaniment of Mr. Redhouse's drum. Enjoyable? Certainly. And serious community activity at the same time!

Several years ago, while walking in Hawaii, I came upon a courtyard where a Japanese Bon Festival (the Buddhist feast of all souls, or midsummer's celebration) was beginning. Musicians played and sang from the top of a tower in the center of the courtyard while the community danced in concentric circles around its base. Everyone who could walk, danced. Those who could not walk were carried and "danced" by those who could. After sitting and watching for several hours, I was invited to join the dance. Unable to communicate verbally with anyone in the group, I seldom have felt more at home than I did that night. In both the Indian and the Buddhist dance, I experienced a sense of inclusiveness, of embracing all of life in a manner which was at once simple and profound, natural, and available to all.

In 1981, I was privileged to direct — and finally be swept along by — a wonderfully primitive recessional dance at the Motherhouse and Healthcare Center of the Sisters of St. Francis in Rochester, Minnesota. Even wheelchairs and canes were no obstacle to the dance. When the music began, all moved. Some rode and sang and danced with their arms, others pushed and danced with their feet, and the entire assembly proceeded at a pace *all* could keep.

The Indian and Buddhist dances and the recessional dance at the Franciscan Motherhouse shared one important, identifying characteristic of primitive dance: unity. There were no distinctions made between performer and audience, no questions raised about whether the activity was esthetic or utilitarian, whether it was prayer or work or pleasure. All present were participants. The dancing was beautiful and served a purpose. It was prayer and work and pleasure. When questions and distinctions of the above sort appear in primitive practice, they are often interpreted as signs of weakening in the community's life. "As soon as a rite . . . becomes a mere spectacle, seeking to influence man rather than commune with God, its universal power is broken and it disintegrates. Religion separates itself from dance, and art from work; the sacred becomes profane entertainment; and old rituals . . . degenerate."[2]

Most dance in our present time and culture has drifted far from its primitive origins. Torn from contact with the whole of life, it has for the most part been reduced to show and eroticism. Even folk dance, which has preserved much original and deeply religious material, is often now practiced as a diversion from life rather than an expression of the fabric of life.

Christians who claim the primitive dance experience will claim many treasures. They will claim their oneness with people who view all of life (and each individual life) as a unified, sacred reality. They will come to accept that universal ground of human expression, bodily movement, as the ground on which they too stand. They will realize that the enmity between religion and dance has come from the profaning of dance, not from the incompatibility of the movement of the human spirit and the movement of the temple in which that spirit lives. They will come to joyfully proclaim that, as believers in the Incarnation of God and in themselves as embodied spirit and enspirited flesh, they can and must dance.

Approaching movement expression through the primitive experience will also help to liberate Christian individuals and communities from the pain of self-consciousness and from the danger of "show." The primitive does not dance for an audience, but for God and for the good of the community of which he or she is an integral part. The Christian celebrant or liturgical dancer cannot perform for an audience because "there is no audience . . . in the liturgical celebration. This fact alone distinguishes it from most other public assemblies."[3] The celebrant who hesitates to craft his movement prayer because he does not want to put on a show can be encouraged. He may discover that if his attention is on his movement offering to God and on the community for whose sake he moves, there is no show, but only and truly the possibility of incarnational prayer. The celebrant or dancer who does want to show off (even if only unconsciously) may learn from the primitive mind that there is more to celebrational gesture and dance than that which is seen by human eyes alone.

The primitive mind on dance may at first be confusing to a dancer raised in our twentieth-century Western culture. How can dance exist without a human audience? If there is no audience, what is there for a dancer to do? Further into this volume, the liturgical dance artist's ministry will be examined and defined. At this point, let three examples suffice.

A dancer might lead the Good Friday cross or Gospel book in procession, moving skillfully and reverently in relation to the sacred object, perhaps bearing a candle or a burning censor. Fashioned solely to support the community's prayerful attention on the cross or Word, the movement would be in accord with both the primitive dancer's intention to dance in the name of a praying community and the American bishops' statement that dance can become a meaningful part of the celebration if it "benefits the total liturgical action."[4]

Secondly, a dancer might teach or lead a community's liturgical gesture. Third, he or she might research or create congregational dances, Christian folk dances, to be performed as a prelude to or at the conclusion of the liturgy, at a communal supper, or out in a field at a parish picnic. Examples of all the above are described later in this book. This is not to say that the liturgical dancer may not craft a dance which could be offered, in the same way a choir or soloist might offer a song, as a meditation during the liturgy. It is to say, however, that there is much, much more to liturgical dance ministry than performing.

For the primitive, dance is the primary expression of the unity of body and soul, the unity of persons in community, the unity of religion, art, work, and community life. It is at the same time serious business and joyful celebration. It is holy work and holy play. As Christian movement artists— priest-celebrants and ministers, liturgical dancers, and members of the assembly alike—we have much we can learn from the primitive dance. Deo gratias!

5

From Miriam and David

The history of the early Jewish nation is Christian history. It is the Jewish scriptures which form most of what Christians call the Old Testament. Many of the psalms instruct the faithful Jew to "praise the Lord in his sanctuary . . . with timbrel and dance" (Ps 150), to "join in procession with leafy boughs up to the horns of the altar" (Ps 118), to lift the hands in prayer (Ps 63), to bow down in worship and kneel before the Lord (Ps 95), to sing and shout and clap God's praises (Ps 47). It is impossible to wholeheartedly sing and shout and clap God's praises without moving!

In the fiftieth chapter of Sirach,[1] we find a description of the conclusion of a service at the altar in which ritual movement plays a significant part.

> Once [Simon, the priest] had completed the services
>   at the altar
>
> . . .
>
> The sons of Aaron would sound a blast,
>   the priests, on their trumpets of beaten metal;
>
> . . .
>
> Then all the people with one accord
>   would quickly fall prostrate to the ground
> In adoration before the Most High.
>
> . . .
>
> Then hymns would re-echo,
>
> . . .

All the people of the land would shout for joy,
    praying to the Merciful One,
. . .
Then coming down [the priest] would raise his hands
    over the congregation of Israel.
. . .
Then again the people would lie prostrate
    to receive from him the blessing of the Most High.

Sirach 50: 14-21

Processions, prostrations, encircling of the altar or Torah, bowing, lifting the hands in prayer, swaying, and dancing were all embraced as human actions which assisted the community's prayer to Yahweh. The two most frequently quoted accounts of dancing in the Old Testament are found in Exodus 15 and 2 Samuel 6. In the first, which recounts the delivery of the Israelites from Egypt, Miriam leads the women in a dance of thanksgiving.

> The prophetess Miriam, Aaron's sister, took a tambourine in her hand, while all the women went out after her with tambourines, dancing; and she led them in the refrain:
> > Sing to the Lord, for he is gloriously triumphant;
> > horse and chariot he has cast into the sea.
> > Exod 15: 20-21

We do not have a description of that dance. However, sacred dance historian E. Louis Backman suggests that the dance led by Miriam was a kind of hopping dance.[2] About David's dance, we have more information.

> Then David, girt with a linen apron, came dancing before the Lord with abandon, as he and all the Israelites were bringing up the ark of the Lord with shouts of

joy and to the sound of the horn. As the ark of the Lord
was entering the City of David, Saul's daughter Michal
looked down through the window and saw King David
leaping and dancing before the Lord....

2 Sam 6: 14–16

The words *sāhaq* (dance), *kārar* (whirl about), *pāzaz* (leap),
and *rāqad* (skip) are all used in this passage and give us a
good idea of what David's dance must have been like.[3]

Nowhere in the Old Testament or in Mosaic Law are there
prohibitions against dance. Dance is presented in a negative
light only on those occasions when it is performed to honor
false gods or when it is associated with drunkenness (Exod
32:19). Because of the many mentions of dance in connection
with holy days and festivals, we can presume it was a usual
and integral part of Jewish religious life, a part with which
Jesus would have been well familiar. When we look at the
number of words for dance in the Hebrew language, and at
the number of times these words are used in the Old Testament to describe ritual movement, community dancing, and
the movement of mountains, lambs, seas, rivers, and all creation, we must presume that dance played a natural and vital
role in the life of the Jewish people.

Three Festivals

Three major yearly festivals of the Jewish nation were originally signified by names which indicated that dancing was an
integral part of their observance. *Hāg*, meaning a sacred
round dance, formed part of the earliest names for *Pesāch* or
the Feast of Unleavened Bread (*hag ha-Mazzôth*), *Shabuôth*
or Pentecost (*hag ha-Kazir*) and *Sukkôth* or the Feast of Ingathering (*hag ha-Asiph*).

Pesāch, or Passover, before the enslavement in Egypt, was

a springtime festival celebrating the birth of the new kids and lambs. This festival took place during the night of the full moon in the month nearest the spring equinox, and was characterized by the smearing of the blood of the sacrificial lamb or goat on the entrances to the shepherds' tents to keep away evil spirits, by the partaking of a sacrificial meal, and by the performance of sacred dances.[4] Later, this feast was assumed into the Feast of Unleavened Bread at the time of the barley harvest, and associated with the deliverance of the Hebrew people from Egypt. The word pesāch itself refers to a kind of limping step. The original dance of the shepherds, imitative of the uncertain step of the newborn kid, evolved into the dance of the "newborn" Hebrew slave. Because of the use of the word *hāg* in the description of the pesāch step, we know that this dance was done around an altar of sacrifice.

Shabuôth, or Pentecost, was celebrated seven weeks after Passover at the end of the barley harvest and the beginning of the wheat harvest. It was in later history connected with the renewal of the covenant between Yahweh and his people. One ritual action of this festival was the priest's waving of two loaves of unleavened bread, signifying the offering back to God of the fruits of the earth. Shabuoth was celebrated with joyous feasting followed by the community's performance of religious songs and dances.

Sukkôth, also called the Feast of Tabernacles and the Feast of Ingathering, was an autumn festival. The celebration of Sukkôth involved processional dances to the temple. The first part of Psalm 81 is a processional hymn which was sung at Sukkôth. Upon arrival at the temple, the women waved branches and performed dances in the Women's Court, then gathered in the galleries to watch the men perform their ritual torch dances.

Dances of Victory

Victorious Hebrew warriors were greeted by women who honored them with singing and dancing:

> At the approach of Saul and David [on David's return from slaying the Philistine], women came out from each of the cities of Israel to meet King Saul, singing and dancing, with tambourines, joyful songs and sistrums. The women played and sang:
> "Saul has slain his thousands,
> and David his ten thousands."
>
> 1 Sam 18:6–7

Judges 11:29–40 presents the sad story of Jepthah's daughter who greeted her victorious father "playing the tambourines and dancing," only to lose her life because she was the first one Jepthah encountered upon returning home.

Judith, having saved her people from Holofernes, was acclaimed by women "who performed a dance in her honor," and whom she then led in the dance, "crowned with garlands of olive leaves. . . . The men of Israel followed in their armor, wearing garlands and singing hymns" (Jdt 15:12–13).

Betrothal and Marriage

In Judges 21 we find reference to the betrothal dances of the young women of Israel. Connie Fisher, author of *Dancing the Old Testament*, beautifully describes these dances:

> The daughters of marriageable age were dressed in white. . . . They danced and sang passages from the Songs of Solomon: "Go forth, O daughters of Zion." The young men stood in a group and watched the dancers as they swayed to the rhythm of their song: "Charm is deceitful and beauty is vain, but a woman who fears the Lord is to be praised." One by one, each young man

would step to the group and touch the hand of the young woman he wished to make his wife. This was no frivolous dance, but a solemn ritual, in which a young couple pledged their loyalty and love to one another.[5]

Jewish wedding celebrations, lasting several days, were occasions of great feasting and dancing. A song to accompany a ritual wedding dance is found in the Song of Songs 7:1.

> Turn, turn, O Shulamite,
> turn, turn, that we may look at you!

Ecstatic Dancing

The early prophets of the Old Testament performed a kind of ecstatic dance, arising out of an engendering strong religious emotion and ending in a mystical union with God. It was to these prophets that Samuel sent Saul, telling him, "As you enter [Gibeath-elohim], you will meet a band of prophets, in a prophetic state, coming down from the high place preceded by lyres, tambourines, flutes and harps. The Spirit of the Lord will rush upon you, and you will join them in their prophetic state and will be changed into another man" (1 Sam 10:5-6). Saul's encounter with the dancing prophets was part of his formation for kingship.

Of all the types of dance we find in the Old Testament— ritual movement in the sanctuary, processions, dancing at religious festivals and weddings, and the ecstatic dancing of the prophets—the most problematic to modern minds is the ecstatic dance. One author has gone so far as to entitle one of the chapters in his book *The Prophets of Israel*, "Israel's Prophets Were Not Ecstatics."[6] He asserts this because, for him, use of the word ecstatic to describe Israel's prophets allies them with the false prophets of Baal who used dance for religious self-stimulation and as magic to force the gods to reveal themselves and act on their behalf. The author's concern is understandable. The prophets of the Jewish nation had no need to stimulate either God or themselves. They knew God to be all-powerful, revealing himself when and where he wanted, and not subject to magical conjurings. But nowhere in the Old Testament is it inferred that the ecstatic dance of the Jewish prophets was the same as that of the prophets of Baal.

To assert that Israel's prophets were not ecstatic is to abandon the true meaning of the word ecstasy and to ignore a possible meaning of that word in our experience today. The root of the word ecstatic is the Greek *ekstasis*, meaning literally to be or to stand outside of one's self. All true religious dance is in some sense ecstatic. That is, it permits the dancer the grace of standing outside the self, of becoming momentarily un-self-centered, of emptying the self in order to be filled and moved by God. Gerardus van der Leeuw boldly states that when ecstatic dance is dropped from the religious life of a community, so are abandonment, surrender, and ability to let God be God. He further points to the fragile balance between effort and surrender which must be understood by anyone who would dance for or with God. "The dance, like every other art, demands practice and knowledge. But the dancer who gives the impression that he is executing a well-thought-out plan, instead of surrendering to a power which uses his limbs as willing instruments, is not a true dancer."[7]

Surely David's dance was ecstatic, as were the dances of Miriam, Judith, and Jepthah's daughter. So also the joyous dancing at weddings. Far from being the antithesis of Jewish experience, ecstatic dancing may lie near the heart of it. Embracing that tradition today, we—the celebrant lifting the chalice, the dance artist offering a meditation after Communion, the member of the assembly signing himself or herself with the height and depth and breadth of Christ's cross—may discover the release that comes from being carried by the movement itself, that comes from stepping aside from both self-consciousness and show and being danced!

❧ 6 ❧

Bishop Ambrose and Company

A s a devout Jew, Jesus was well aware of the significance of ritual, prayer-filled movement in the life of God's people. While calling hypocritical those actions and gestures not accompanied by similar movements of the heart (Matt 23:5, 28), he takes for granted that the contrite man will bow his head and beat his breast (Luke 18:9-14).

The writings of the early Church Fathers reflect a continuation of Jesus' concern for a unity of body, mind, and spirit in private and liturgical prayer. Throughout the writings of the Fathers, there are references to postures, gestures, and sacred dances as vehicles for the expression and impression of the holy faith.

Standing

Standing was the normal posture of prayer for the Jews. Jesus says, in Mark 11:25, "When you stand to pray. . . ." He himself would have often prayed in this traditional way, standing, with hands raised.

Standing, to acknowledge the Risen Lord, was the accepted posture of Christians at early celebrations of the Eucharist. Standing, opposed to the more passive posture of sitting, is actually a movement, a continuous process of rising from the earth. It is a movement which expresses attentiveness and alertness. Rising to the standing position is a traditional sign of respect. Tertullian (c. 160–c. 225) chastizes those who sit in church. "If it is disrespectful to sit down in the presence and sight of one whom you hold in very high esteem and honor, how much more is it the height of disrespect to do so in the presence of the living God with the angel of prayer standing beside Him? Unless we are offering a reproach to God because our prayer has wearied us!"[1] Canon 20 of the Council of Nicea reads, "As some kneel on the Lord's day and on the days of Pentecost, the holy Synod has decided that, for the observance of a general rule, all shall offer their prayers to God standing."[2] Clement of Alexandria (c. 150-c. 215) also recommends standing for liturgical prayer, adding that the faithful might raise their hands and head toward heaven, and even stand on tiptoe![3]

Sitting

Sitting at liturgy was limited to the presider, meaning literally "he who sits before," and to the elderly and infirm. Not until the sixteenth century were pews introduced into Christian churches.

Kneeling and Prostrating

Luke reports that Jesus "went down on his knees and prayed" in the Garden of Gethsemane (Luke 22:41). Matthew describes that same moment saying that Jesus "fell prostrate in prayer" (Matt 26:39). In early Christian practice, kneeling was the recommended posture for private prayer and a required public posture for penitents. Kneeling did not become an accepted liturgical gesture for all until the time of the Counter-Reformation with its emphasis on the adoration of Jesus in the Blessed Sacrament exposed. Both Augustine (354–430) and Tertullian, after reminding Christians that standing, facing east, was the proper posture for the assembly's prayer on the Lord's day, recommended the posture of kneeling on other occasions. As regards private prayer, Augustine writes, "Those who pray compose their bodily members in a manner befitting suppliants when they fix their knees, extend their hands and even prostrate themselves."[4] And Tertullian graphically links this posture with the realities of the Christian life in his day. "As we kneel with arms extended to God, let the hooks dig into us, let the crosses suspend us, the fires lick us, the swords cut our throats, and wild beasts leap upon us: the very posture of a Christian in prayer makes him ready for every punishment."[5] He directs that prayers on fast and station days "be said on the knees with every other sign of a humble spirit."[6]

Genuflection

Genuflection is a problematic gesture. The earliest Church Fathers would not have recommended it because it was originally a gesture of adoration made to a pagan god or an earthly ruler. However, by the time of Constantine, genuflection had taken on a tone merely of respect, and the Church allowed the emperor to be honored by this gesture. Bishops too, who under Constantine were recognized both as holy men and as persons of state, were greeted with genuflection both inside and outside the house of God. The Church also soon encouraged the faithul to use this same gesture to honor objects which indeed were holy yet not deserving of adoration, such as the altar, relics, and the images of saints. Genuflection did not take on the meaning of veneration and adoration for Christians until after the eighth century.[7]

Raising the Hands

"The heavens are my throne" (Isa 66:1). Raising the hands toward the throne of God was a natural gesture among the Jews. That it was also a Christian gesture of prayer directed to

Jesus seated at the right hand of the throne of God is witnessed by the images, called *orantes*, found on the walls of the catacombs. In his first letter to Timothy, Paul writes, "It is my wish, then, that in every place the men shall offer prayers with blameless hands held aloft, and be free from anger and dissension" (1 Tim 2:8).

St. Clement of Rome (fl. c. 96) writes to the Corinthians, "Let us come before Him, then, in sanctity of soul, lifting pure and undefiled hands to Him."[8] Tertullian declares "not only do we raise [our hands], we even spread them out, and, imitating the Passion of our Lord, we confess Christ as we pray."[9] However, Tertullian cautions that the hands, and also the eyes, must never be raised in presumption.[10]

Sign of the Cross

A small sign of the cross, made on the eyes or forehead, and much later a large sign to trace on one's body the very height, depth, and breadth of Christ's redemptive act, was believed to be a significant prayer which had sacramental power. Tertullian exhorted believers to make the sign of the cross to accompany each movement of daily life. Augustine felt that "unless the sign of the cross was made on the foreheads of the faithful, as on the water wherewith they were regenerated, or on the oil with which they were anointed with chrism, or on the sacrifice with which they were nourished, none of these things was duly performed."[11]

Laying On of Hands

Jesus laid his hands on people to heal and bless them. This gesture was continued by Jesus' followers as they prayed in Jesus' name. In Acts 13:3, the gesture of laying on of hands accompanies the commissioning of Saul and Barnabas. In Acts 19:6, Paul lays his hands on the disciples at Ephesus (who had already received the baptism of John) that they might be baptized in the name of Jesus and receive the Holy Spirit. In Acts 9:17, Ananias lays his hands on Saul that Saul might recover his sight, receive the Holy Spirit, and be prepared for ministry. In Acts 28:8, Publicus's father is healed by Paul's praying and laying hands on him.

In the centuries of the Christian Church that followed, the gesture of laying on of hands signified many things including "blessing, setting apart, consecrating, commissioning, absolving, healing, confirming, declaring [and] ordaining."[12]

Striking the Breast

Striking the breast, a gesture of sorrow for sin, the root of which was thought to be found in the heart or breast, was recommended by St. Augustine.[13] An old picture of St. Jerome (c. 342–420) shows him kneeling in the desert, striking his breast with a stone. "It is an honest blow, not an elegant gesture," and signifies a hammering against the fortresses of the heart in order to open them to grace.[14]

Sign of Peace

Recognizing the impressive as well as the expressive power of the movement, Augustine advised the faithful to "give [the sign of peace] and receive it in such a way that you will have charity."[15] Tertullian criticized those who refrained from offering the sign while they were fasting. "This [sign] is the seal of prayer," he said, and our prayer is "made more worthy of praise because of our charity."[16] He went so far as to say that no liturgical service was complete without the kiss of peace.

The form of the kiss was probably not a kiss on the mouth or cheek. That would have been considered too familiar. Depending on place, period, or status, one would have kissed another's hand or even foot or knee. Equals bent to kiss each other's shoulder. This latter form is still practiced in some religious orders and between concelebrants in the Byzantine liturgy.[17]

Dance

St. Gregory of Nyssa (c. 330–395) indicated that David's dance before the Ark of the Lord signified "intense joy" and outwardly manifested the state of his soul.[18] St. Ambrose (339–97) praised David's dance and corrected those who would criticize it. David

> played before the Lord as His servant and pleased Him the more in so humbling himself before God and laying aside his royal dignity. . . . Let one who still doubts hear the testimony of the Gospel, for the Son of God says: "We have played for you, and you have not danced." . . . These actions of the body, though unseemly when viewed in themselves, become reverential under the aspect of holy religion, so that those who censure them drag their own souls into the net of censure. Thus Michal censured David for dancing and said: "How glorious was the king of Israel today, for he uncovered himself today before the eyes of his handmaids." And David answered her: "I will play before the Lord who chose me rather than my father, and then all his house, and commanded me to be ruler over his people of Israel."[19]

One of the passages relating to the actual performance of dance during the divine service comes from Justin the Martyr (c. 100–c. 165). "It is not for the little ones to sing alone, but rather together with musical instruments and dancing and rattles, just in the same way as one enjoys songs and similar music in church."[20] This children's dancing during liturgy was later taken over by boys' choirs.

Sts. John Chrysostom, Theodoret, and others observed

that sacred round dances in the churches not only created a sense of joy and unity in those who participated, but also enabled the dancers to reflect on earth the dances of the saints and angels around the heavenly throne of God. "For God," says Chrysostom, "has not given us our feet to use in a shameful way . . . but in order to dance ring-dances with the angels."[21] The ring-dance in the choir of the church, combined with the holy ritual, enabled the faithful to "dance with and in imitation of the invisible angels."[22]

Writing to St. Gregory of Nyssa, St. Gregory Nazianzus (329–89) described the manner in which the feasts of martyrs should be celebrated. "If we assemble to celebrate this festival in such a way that it shall be agreeable to Christ and at the same time honour the martyrs, then we must execute our triumphant ring-dance. . . . Great throngs of people must perform a ring-dance for the martyrs in reverent honour of the precious blood."[23] St. Gregory of Nazianzus begged the Emperor Julian to abandon the dissolute dances and to "dance to the honor of God" and in a manner that is "worthy of an emperor and a Christian."[24] St. John Chrysostom (345–407) praised the Christians of Constantinople for their celebrations of the Feast of the Holy Ghost. "You have passed the greater part of the day together in transports of moderation, in the performance of ring-dances in the spirit of St. Paul. By this your merits have increased doubly, in the first place because you refrained from the indecent dances of the drunken, and in the second place because you danced those spiritual dances which are most pleasing and most modest."[25] St. Chrysostom records that bishops were the leaders of the sacred church dances.[26]

St. Ambrose, commenting on Luke 7:32, wrote that "the dance should be conducted as did David when he danced before the ark of the Lord, for everything is right which springs from the fear of God."[27] Referring to the same passage at another time, he said:

> For that reason we have announced to you the rejoicing in heaven, and you may lift up your hearts in rapture. For this reason the Lord bids us to dance, not merely with the circling movements of the body, but with pious faith in him. For just as he who dances with his body at one time floats ecstatically, at another leaps in the air and at another by varying degrees pays reverence to certain places, so also he who dances in the spirit with a burning faith is carried aloft, is uplifted to the stars, and at the same time solemnly glorifies Heaven by the dances of the thought of Paradise. And just as he who dances with his body, rushing through the rotating movements of the limbs, acquires the right to share in the round dance—in the same way he who dances the spiritual dance, always moving in the ecstacy of faith, acquires the right to dance in the ring of all creation.[28]

Commenting on Psalm 47:2, St. Ambrose said "What did [David] mean by singing: 'Clap your hands all you people'? Obviously, if we consider his bodily actions, we realize that he clapped his hands, dancing. . . ."[29]

The Fathers wrote also about the instrument of dance, the body. St. Gregory of Nyssa wrote that undue preoccupation with the body is neither helpful to prayer nor commended by Scripture.[30] But St. Basil reminded his readers that the body, united as it is with the soul, cannot be neglected without dire consequences to prayer.[31] And Augustine addressed those who would disparage the body, saying that to do so is to disparage the Creator.[32]

The Fathers were united in criticizing dances which were performed to entertain and to elicit human praise, rather than to bring honor to God. Augustine even advised against

baptizing any theatrical dancer who might seek the sacrament.[33] The Fathers were critical of communal dances—even
in the church yards on the feasts of martyrs or saints—which
were accompanied by drunkenness and the singing of shameful songs.

It seems apparent from their writing that the early Church
Fathers desired Christians to claim their bodies as temples of
the Holy Spirit, to form attitudes of body that conformed
with attitudes of heart, to dance to honor God, to imitate the
angels, and to outwardly and unashamedly proclaim with
their dancing their faith in God who has come in the body.

✄ 7 ✄

Full Circle

Although it may be an oversimplification, it is neverthe-
less true to say that between the time of the early Church
Fathers to the time of the Second Vatican Council, there was
in the Church and in the world of dance a movement from
activity to spectacle, from actual involvement to vicarious involvement, from active participation to passive observation.

In the classical shape of the liturgy, clergy and lay alike
were active participants, equal in importance, differing in
order, charism, or function. "The apostolic and primitive
church regarded the eucharist as primarily an *action*, something 'done,' not something 'said'; and . . . it had a clear and
unhesitating grasp of the fact that this action was *corporate*,
the united joint action of the whole church and not of the
celebrant only."[1] After the conversion of Constantine, when
Christianity became a state religion, clergy became persons of
state, above the laity at least in civil importance. The Church
grew and spread through missionary activity, and this increase
caused changes in liturgical praxis. What had been small
gatherings in domestic settings became large gatherings in
quite public settings. The liturgy which the people had first
known as their own work and action in intimate cooperation
with the redemptive work and action of God and his ministers,
became a work to watch others do in their behalf, an action
performed by the clergy, effective without their assistance.

In the seventh and eighth centuries, because of the grow-

ing number of priests in monasteries and their desire to celebrate the liturgy daily rather than on the Lord's day alone,
another phenomenon appeared. Priests said "private Masses,"
attended by a server but not by a congregation. Influenced
by this development within the monasteries, secular priests
began reciting "low Masses," attended only by a server, and
leaving the congregation to simply watch and listen. Prayers
said "in secret," in an inaudible voice, finally left little for an
assembled people to do save utter private prayers of their
own.

In the classical shape of the liturgy, there had been a "good
deal of moving about" by an actively involved community
and its ministers.[2] The development of private and low Masses
caused that good deal of moving about to be reduced to a few
steps by the priest from the center of the altar to the credence
table at its right or from the "epistle side" to the "gospel side"
of the altar.[3] That movement eventually became elaborated
with a multiplication of gestures given allegorical meaning:
repeated genuflections, strikings of the breast, kissing of the
altar or the missal. The high point of this Dance was the ele-
vation of the sacred Host at the Consecration. People often
ran from church to church to watch this moment of the Dance
without ever coming to receive Communion. Indeed, by the
ninth century, it had become such common practice for the
priest alone to receive Communion that it was necessary to
establish a rule that all lay persons "must communicate once
a year at Easter at the least."[4]

Despite the general trend toward less and less involvement
on the part of the assembly, there is scattered evidence of
quite moving involvement. A Gallican sacramentary of the
seventh century contains a Eucharistic prayer which reads in
part: "We beseech thee, almighty Father, eternal God, de-
liver us from all temptation, give us help in every conflict. . . .

Grant that we may worship thee with a pure heart; let us dance before thee with a clean conscience; let us serve thee with all our strength."[5] A tenth-century hymnal from the monastery of Moissac contains the following hymn, to be sung at Mass on Easter morning:

> His [Christ's] life, His speech and miracles,
> His wondrous death prove it.
> The congregation adorns the sanctity
> Come and behold the host of ring-dances![6]

Also during this time, we find official encouragement of a liturgical dance group. In the seventh century, the Council of Toledo suggested to Isidore, the archbishop of Seville, that he create a ritual which would be distinguished by reverent and beautiful choreography. The result was incorporated into the Mozarabic rite, celebrated in the seven churches of Toledo, and seen even today in the Cathedral of Seville. Margaret Fisk Taylor describes the dance of *los seises* ("the six"):

> This *Mozarbe* with the dances of *los mozos de coro* (chor-isters) became known and authorized as the mass which included the dances of *los seises* according to a bull of Pope Eugenius IV in 1439. At that time, *los seises* (origi-nally six choirboys) danced before the ark on the altar and were "dressed as angels." The costume was composed of short, wide britches of a Moorish cut; a short, sleeveless mantle; a tight-fitting jacket; wreaths of intertwined flowers worn on the bare head; and gilded wings affixed to the shoulders. Thus the dancing choristers really repre-sented the angels in heaven who had descended to the church choir in order to continue there the dance of the blessed in paradise—quite similar to the writings of Clement of Alexandria in A.D. 195. Later, in the Renais-sance, the costume of a page was adopted and this is the

costume still worn today. The choirboys wear red coats, short yellow britches, red stockings, and hats with plumes.[7]

Toward the end of the seventeenth century, the dancing of *los seises* was condemned by Archbishop Palafox of Seville. Amazed at the condemnation, the inhabitants of Seville raised enough money to send the boys to Rome to dance for the pope. The pope reportedly said, "I see nothing in this children's dance which is offensive to God. Let them continue to dance before the high altar."[8] The boys did continue to dance, on the Feast of the Immaculate Conception, on Shrove Tuesday, and in the presence of the Blessed Sacrament on Corpus Christi. The music which accompanied their dancing varied on different occasions and in different ages. One visitor to the Cathedral in 1690 reported the following song:

> (*standing still*)
> We believe in the bread of life
> From Christ to our overflowing joy;
> By our dance we supplicate him,
> As once the Baptist supplicated.
> (*dancing*)
> Therefore by this dance
> We strengthen our firm faith,
> All to the sounds of music![9]

There is evidence of much church dancing by the people and clergy during the Middle Ages and the Renaissance. We will examine here three dances which took place in church, and even in the sanctuary.

Labyrinth Dances

As early as the fourth century, but notably after the eleventh century, labyrinth designs were often laid in the floors of cathedrals. The Church labyrinth was reminiscent of the legendary one of Crete which was trod by Theseus. Theseus entered the labyrinth in order to slay the Minotaur and to lead those who were held captive back out to life. In the Church, the Minotaur became identified with Satan, Theseus with Christ, and the labyrinthian journey with Christ's descent into the underworld to save those held captive there. Margaret Fisk Taylor quotes the following account of a labyrinth dance in a church in 1478:

> Thereafter comes the solemn procession in memory of the procession which Christ . . . solemnized when he returned from the underworld, leading out those he had delivered into the paradise of ecstacy, dancing and hopping. He introduces both music and dance in consideration of the liberation of so many souls. He sings to them a song which none should utter except to God's immortal Son after his wondrous triumph. And we all, happy and adorned with spiritual perfection, follow our highest master, who himself leads the solemn ring dance.[10]

At times, the Church labyrinth served pilgrims who, unable to go to Jerusalem because of its occupation by the unfaithful, walked or crawled along its passages as if on "The road to Jerusalem."[11] As late as 1929, it was reported that visitors to the Cathedral at Chartres still practiced the devotion of the rosary on the labyrinth.[12] In a 1983 issue of *Parabola*, P.L. Travers speaks of visiting that very cathedral and its maze. Her comments reveal that much of the original Christian interpretation of the maze—and the dance associated with it —has been lost:

> Not long ago, a geometer friend of mine invited me and some of his pupils to go to Chartres and walk the Maze while he took measurements—a cardinal privilege, for

in recent centuries, among the clerics of the Cathedral,
the Labyrinth has been held to be a pagan symbol, one
to be discreetly secluded from the laity lest their temple
be profaned.... They have even wiped from their
minds, these same clerics, the part of their ancient liturgy
that required the Bishop, at Eastertide, to lead the
Round Dance through the Labyrinth; to say nothing of
the fact that it was incumbent upon every pilgrim to
tread it — perhaps as a form of initiation — before he approached the altar. [13]

Today, at St. Nicholas Center here in Tucson, one finds
painted on one of the walls a Yaqui "Man in a Maze," a modern labyrinth, image of an ancient religious dance.

The Pelota

The *pelota* was a dance performed on the labyrinth by priests
and newly inducted canons at Eastertime in many places in
France. A ball, large enough to be held in both hands, was
passed from dancer to dancer as the group moved along the
labyrinth's path, singing the Easter hymn *Victimi Paschali
laudes*. Since the group at times circled the labyrinth, and at
times individuals turned on their own axes, all the while passing the ball among themselves, the dance is thought to repre-
sent the movement of the sun throughout the year, and therefore its "passion." [14]

The pelota was a dance of the clergy. The further we come
from the time of the early Church Fathers, the more we see
dances of the clergy alone and of the people alone. Dance is a
great equalizer of persons. Although St. John Chrysostom
can record that in the fourth century bishops led their people
in the Church dances, soon after that, the clergy, in order to
claim and maintain their superior position in the Church,
danced by themselves separate from the people.

Ecternach

The hopping dance and processional to the church of St. Willibrord in Luxembourg dates from the fourteenth century and continues even now in the twentieth century. The procession, led by the priests and those carrying banners, large candles and a processional cross, and followed by up to several thousands of dancing pilgrims and children, begins just outside the town of Ecternach and makes it way to the church in the town. Upon entering the church, "the procession dances in on the so-called evangelical side, i.e., the right aisle. It continues dancing up to the choir and the high altar. Many burst into tears at the sight of the tomb of the saint. They kneel at the altar, embrace it, kiss its walls and lay rose wreaths, medals, pictures and books upon it. Then they continue the hopping dance round the altar and back by the epistolary aisle, i.e., the left aisle. Then the dance proceeds out of the church into the surrounding churchyard, three times circling the large cross."[15] The following hymn accompanies the dance:

> In honour of Christ
> On this day
> Celebrate everywhere
> All the faithful
> With great dances (*magna tripudio*)
> And deepest reverence
> The wonderful father
> Saint Willibrordus.[16]

Gerardus van der Leeuw, commenting on procession and on the many historical occasions of procession in the Christian Church, warns us not to consider the procession as something other than a dance. It is, rather, a line dance. The Corpus Christi procession has long been a tradition in the Church. Taylor writes that these "processions were originally nothing more than ambulatory dances in which the participants, following a certain pattern, bowed in measure, swung censors in cadence, and threw flowers into the air."[17]

Processions like the ones to remember St. Willibrord and to honor the Blessed Sacrament set a whole community in motion. Because most church processions are now performed by the ministers alone, the only contemporary counterpart to the ones mentioned above is the demonstration or march. Those who have taken part in demonstrations or marches have been known to comment that participation was for them a "religious experience." For good reason. An entire "community of faith" has been joined in one unified dance of faith! The Passion Sunday procession with palms still remains, in print, as a procession of the entire community. However, I would dare to say that the majority of churches now pass out palms to people in their pews and invite only a representative few to move in procession. Logical, practical reasons are given for keeping the congregation in the pews. A procession of the entire congregation would take too much time (people won't come if they think the Mass will take any longer than usual, and the parking lot might not be cleared in time for the next Mass), too much organization (who would get everyone in line?), too messy (who is going to pick up the palm fronds that the children drop along the way?). And so the congregation is kept in its place, in its role of spectator.

In addition to the labyrinth, *pelota*, and processional dances, there was much ceremonial dancing in the churches and churchyards at weddings, baptisms, ordinations, and on major feasts throughout the Middle Ages and Renaissance.

During the Middle Ages, orders of priests and nuns found dancing helpful to the prayer and worship of their disciplined groups. Fra Jacopone da Todi, a Franciscan monk, wrote "O, that each one who loves the Lord would join in the dance singing of his devotion."[18] The nuns at Villaceaux celebrated the feasts of the Holy Innocents and Mary Magdalene with dancing. By the Renaissance, images of movement and dance appeared in works of art made for churches. Donatello Botticelli, and Fra Angelo depict in their paintings the angels, saints, and redeemed dancing in paradise. Michelangelo and others began to sculpt the human form in motion rather than in the static positions so common until then.

Not all church dancing, however, qualified as "sacred." From the beginning there were excesses and abuses that led to official censure. In 539, the Council of Toledo forbid dancing in the churchyards on vigils of saints and on days of penance. Toward the end of that century, King Childebert II circulated a letter which forbid dancing, singing, and drunkenness during the night watches of the great Church feasts.[19] From this period on, Church councils sought to end the church dances which led to wrestling, drunkenness, the singing of bawdy songs, and the playing of games which gave rise to quarreling and even murder![20] The Council of Toledo in 633 expressly ruled against the "shameless" songs and dances of the Feast of Fools, a popular festival of either pagan origins or a mixture of "low-level vulgarian Christianity and crass magical conceptions."[21]

While the Church was critical of secular dancing and abuses in church dancing, she was at the same time creating her own dance. Liturgical ritual became more and more elaborate. Processionals, mystery, and morality plays and ceremonial dances abounded. The evidence seems to indicate that it was not dance in the service of the Church which was in question, but dance which made use of the art of movement merely to seek physical pleasure or worldly adulation.

The late sixteenth and seventeenth centuries witnessed both the Council of Trent with its clear impact on liturgical developments, and the growing importance of the court ballet and its impact on the art of movement. The printing of the Roman Breviary (1568), Missal (1570), Pontifical (1596) and Ritual (1614) ended the history of the development of ritual in the Catholic Church until the Second Vatican Council (with the notable exception of the work done in places like Solesmes). What flexibility there had been in the rites, even though those rites had been performed by the clergy alone, was now gone. Every movement and gesture was exactly defined by rubric. Life-filled forms were replaced by formalism.

Lest we be too critical of Trent, let us remember that the Council of Trent was the council of a Church under attack from within and without. Heresies and abuses, many of which concerned liturgical practice, abounded. Before the invention of the printing press, copies of liturgies and prayers were made by hand. Many copy errors were made, and many versions of liturgies produced. With the invention of the printing press, the Council was able to do what it believed necessary to bring order out of chaos, that is, print one official, reformed missal. That the Council did not have access to some of the earliest records of liturgical development and therefore canonized in their reformed missal some practices foreign to the early Church Fathers is not to discredit its efforts. It did the best it could in the circumstances in which it found itself. It was the Council of Trent which produced the liturgy which Ronald Knox called "a kind of ritual dance,"[22] and which two other noted scholars point to as no less than a dance:

> It is everywhere assumed in the literature of the liturgy
> . . . but almost nowhere else in the church that ceremo-
> nial is the art of the body, which is why Newman de-
> scribed the movements of the ministers at high mass as
> "sacred dance."[23]

> There is nothing more beautiful than a High Mass, a
> dance before the Ark in slow motion, more majestic
> than the advance of the hosts of Heaven. And yet the
> Church, in the Mass, is not searching for beauty or deco-
> rative motifs or a means of touching the heart. Her sole
> object is worship and union with her Savior, and from
> this loving worship an excess of beauty overflows.[24]

In the world of dance, from the fifteenth to the seventeenth
centuries, we find developments which are parallel to developments in the liturgy during the same time. Beginning in
the fifteenth but firmly entrenched by the seventeenth century, "we have perhaps for the first time in world history a
clear and strong division between the active and the passive
in human culture, between creators and spectators, between
artist and audience. In the dance this means the growing
importance of the ballet.... The gay pastime of carefree
amateurs [becomes] the serious work of professional dancers."
Former participants become paying audience. Free, natural
expression gives way to rigidity and artificiality.[25] It is perhaps
because of the history of ballet as spectacle in courtly society
and on theatrical stages that the author of a recent essay from
the Congregation for the Sacraments and Divine Worship says:

> Neither can acceptance be had of the proposal to intro-
> duce into the liturgy the so-called artistic ballet because
> there would be presentation here also of a spectacle at
> which one would assist, while in the liturgy one of the
> norms from which one cannot prescind is that of par-
> ticipation.[26]

The dance which is to serve the liturgy of Vatican II must
truly involve the congregation and its ministers in the actual
movement of the dance or it must be performed in such a way

that it can be received kinesthetically and not only visually by the congregation, and that it never leave the congregation in the role of mere onlooker.

It would be helpful to note that at this point in history it is not only the ballet which has isolated itself to a stage and has in fact formed its very movement vocabulary to be seen as if from a stage. Many forms of dance have now followed ballet's lead. The liturgical dancer today, if he or she is not to prescind from the norm of active participation, must find ways of *being with* and sometimes leading the people in the dance and in The Dance. This requires an orientation of heart and technique almost unknown to the conventional dance world. It requires a natural vocabulary of movement with no presumption or artificiality,[27] movement which bears meaning rather than just demonstrates pretty form, movement which joins the dancer — in heart and mind if not also in body — with the assembled worshipers rather than isolating the dancer as performer.

We are about to come full circle with the liturgy as Dance and with the art of movement which might serve The Dance. The liturgy as Dance has gone from activity to spectacle, and is now returning to community activity. The art of movement, which began as "sacred act and priestly office . . . a very serious activity of the entire tribe,"[28] then moved into theatrical spectacle, is now challenged to return to its roots. The "dance before the Ark" goes on, but now responsibility for that Dance lies not only on the shoulders of the ministers, but on the whole people of God as well. All are called to take part in the ceremony, the art, the loving worship in bodily movement and gesture. The liturgical dance artist's task at this time is to facilitate this involvement and to recreate a dance art which is truly prayer and which is woven as a thread into the very fabric of The Dance.

⚭ 8 ⚭

What Do the Documents Say?

Throughout Church documents issued since Vatican II, there is a call for the full, active, and conscious participation of the Christian community gathered for worship. There is a call for the union of interior intention with clear and meaningful outer form in liturgical prayer. The *Constitution on the Sacred Liturgy*, promulgated in 1963, invites the faithful to participation "both internally and externally," and challenges pastors of souls to be zealous and patient enablers of that participation (art. 19). Article 30 of the *Constitution* encourages participation "by means of acclamations, responses, psalmody, antiphons, songs, as well as by actions, gestures and bodily attitudes," and by appropriate times of silence.

Since that document was issued, much effort has gone into developing the acclamations, responses, psalmody, antiphons, and songs of the community and its leaders. Little or no effort has been put into eliciting or shaping liturgical actions, gestures, and bodily attitudes. That liturgical leaders have overlooked or ignored the exhortation to actions, gestures, and bodily attitudes is reflected even in a commentary by the highly esteemed scholar Josef Jungmann: "Article 30 is devoted to the congregation of the faithful and names the elements of its external participation. They range from acclamation, which was a particularly popular form of people's participation in antiquity, to psalmody and hymns."[1]

Since 1963, the importance of bodily movement and posture in prayer has been stressed over and over again. The *General Instruction on the New Roman Missal* (1969) calls for participation "of mind and body" (art. 3), and encourages actions and postures which foster the inner spirit (art. 20). That document points to the unity of the community which "is especially evident in the common postures and actions observed by all the faithful" (art. 62).

Music in Catholic Worship (1971) reminds us that "we are celebrating when we involve ourselves meaningfully in the . . . gestures of the worshiping community" (art. 3), and points out that "no other single factor affects the liturgy as much as the attitude, style, and bearing of the celebrant" (art. 20). Article 5 of that document assures us of the power of those signs and symbols of worship which give bodily expression to our faith, and which in turn nourish and stimulate that faith (art. 5).

The *Directory for Masses with Children* (1973) calls gestures, postures, and action "very important . . . in view of the nature of liturgy as an activity of the entire man" (art. 33), and calls for children's involvement in movement and gesture and, at appropriate times, in the procession at the entrance, Gospel acclamation, offertory, and Communion (art. 34).

The *Instruction on Eucharistic Worship* (1967) invites bishops to consider processions with the Blessed Sacrament involving the entire congregation on feasts such as Corpus Christi (art. 59).

In *Environment and Art in Catholic Worship* (1978), there is a section entitled "The Arts and the Body Language of the Liturgy" which states that "common gestures" must be performed with "an uncommon sensitivity," and that the gestures of the presiding minister have the power to either engage or isolate the community. It argues that "processions and interpretations through bodily movement (dance) can become meaningful parts of the liturgical celebration if done by truly competent persons in the manner that benefits the total liturgical action," and that "worship space must allow for movement" (arts. 55, 56, 59).

Four of the six documents mentioned above—the *Constitution on the Sacred Liturgy*, the *General Instruction on the New Roman Missal*, the *Instruction on Eucharistic Worship*, and the *Directory for Masses with Children*—were issued by the Holy See. *Music in Catholic Worship* and *Environment and Art in Catholic Worship* were produced by the American bishops out of their awareness that authentic liturgical renewal requires more than just attention to words, that it also requires attention to the movements, sights, and sounds of the liturgy that can carry the worshiper beyond words.

The documents call for beauty and naturalness in all the movements which will serve the liturgy. The assembly "cannot be satisfied with anything less than the *beautiful* in its . . . movements."[2] The celebrant's movement must be natural as well as reverent.[3] The dancer must orient his or her work "toward the infinite beauty of God . . . [with] the single aim of turning men's minds devoutly towards God,"[4] and must avoid all pretence.[5]

In 1975, the Congregation for the Sacraments and Divine Worship published an essay in *Noticiae II* which, when it appeared in the newsletter of the Bishop's Committee on the Liturgy in the summer of 1982, caused some consternation among those who understand the power of beauty-filled gesture and the art of movement in liturgy. The essay, "commended for study by diocesan liturgical commissions and offices of worship," was intended as a "point of reference for . . . discussion of dance in the liturgy, but was quickly seized upon by some as a prohibition of all movement and dance. Although the *Noticiae* essay is not an official document, it deserves attention here both for the concern it created when it appeared and for its content. It is the opinion of this author that the essay offers a positive and supportive foundation for dance as a liturgical art, but then negates the possibility of such an art in the Western Church. Here are some excerpts from that essay:

> The dance can be an art . . . which by means of the body, expresses human feelings.
>
> The dance can turn into prayer which expresses itself with a movement which engages the whole being, soul and body. Generally, when the spirit raises itself to God in prayer, it also involves the body.
>
> Among the mystics, we find intervals of dancing as an expression of the fulness of their love for God.
>
> When the Angelic Doctor wished to represent paradise, he represented it as a dance executed by angels and saints.
>
> One can speak of a prayer of the body.
>
> [Speaking of primitives, the essay states]
> Among them, when there is question of worship, the spoken word becomes a chant, and the gesture of going or walking towards the divinity transforms itself into a dance step.
>
> [In reference to Hebrew prayer]
> Such is the case of the Israelites: in the synagogue their prayer is accompanied by a continuous movement to recall the precept from tradition: "When you pray, do so with all your heart, and all your bones."
>
> [Speaking of the Early Church Fathers]
> There is a mention of dancing, an evaluation of it, a comment on the biblical text in which there is an allu-

sion to the dance; more frequently there is a condemnation of profane dances and the disorders to which those dances give rise.

In a comment on Conciliar decisions and writings, the essay points out that, theoretically, the dance might serve Catholic worship, and offers two conditions which would have to precede its acceptance:

The first: to the extent in which the body is a reflection of the soul, dancing, with all its manifestations, would have to express sentiments of faith and adoration in order to become a prayer.

The second condition: just as all the gestures and movements found in the liturgy are regulated by the competent ecclesiastical authority, so also dancing as a gesture would have to be under its discipline.

These two criteria, reflective of the *Constitution on the Sacred Liturgy*, articles 112–129, would set standards for sacred dance equal to the standards the Church sets for sacred music, sacred art and sacred furnishings.

The essay states that a liturgical art of movement, still practiced in the Syriac, Ethiopian, and Byzantine traditions, is possible because those traditions are part of cultures where "dancing is still a reflection of religious values and becomes a clear manifestation of them." The essay goes on to say that in our Western culture, "dancing is tied with love, with diversion, with profaneness," and is exhibitionistic rather than participatory. The fact of the matter is that that is, at least in part, the truth. Christian dance artists, priest-celebrants, and members of the assembly who wish to offer beautiful movement to God face a challenge. The separation of dance, religion, and community life in our culture developed over a long period of time. Reunion is possible, but can come about only through patient reeducation of the Christian assembly and its ministers, and through continuously critical but loving attention to the art of dance which might serve the Church.

Unfortunately, the many positive aspects of the *Noticiae* essay are overshadowed by several weak statements and, finally, by its negative conclusions. The statements that the early Church Fathers make "a mention of dancing" and that there is "an allusion to the dance" in Scripture are highly misleading. As we have already seen, there are many references to festive and ceremonial dance in Scripture, and a good number of the early Church Fathers encouraged Christians to worship God and to celebrate the Church's high feasts with dance.

The statement near the middle of the essay that dancing in the church building "always took place outside of liturgical services," ignores much evidence to the contrary. This includes Justin Martyr's invitation to children's dancing at liturgy, the inclusion of the dance of *los seises* in the Mozarbic Mass, the many references in early hymnals to sacred ringdances at Easter morning Mass, and the processional dances on Corpus Christi and other feasts. There is even a Eucharistic prayer that calls for dancing before the Lord with a pure heart and clean conscience.

Two recommendations at the end of the essay seem unfortunate, based on the history of dance in the Church:

> If the proposal of the *religious dance* in the West is really to be made welcome, care will have to be taken that in its regard a place be found . . . in assembly areas which are not strictly liturgical. Moreover, the priests must always be excluded from the dance.

First, there is a rich history of ceremonial dance outside the liturgy but in liturgical spaces. To state that a Christian community, if it is to dance, must dance in a space other than that in which it prays is to separate the movement of the spirit from the movement of the temple in which that spirit lives, a separation which is obviously detrimental to an incarnational faith-community. Secondly, the admonition that priests are not to take part in the dance seems to echo the concern of centuries past that priests, in order to maintain a separate and superior position, not take part in the same ceremonial dances as the lay folk.

The statement that "here [in our Western culture] dancing is tied with love, with diversion, with profaneness, with unbridling of the senses," is only partially true. The essay does not consider, for example, the many Mexican and Native American dances which are of such spiritual integrity that they are frequently incorporated into the liturgy to the benefit of all. Neither does it recognize the efforts of devout, dedicated clergy and dance artists who are working to restore the liturgy to its rightful place as the liturgical dance par excellence, to cultivate natural, genuine, and beautiful liturgical gesture on the part of ministers and the assembly, and to create an art of movement which can truly and humbly serve The Dance.

The essay finally gives in to the contemporary secular world's definition of dance, rather than pointing to the sacred roots of dance and turning to the power of Christ to redeem, transform, and use the art of movement for the glory of God. Far more in accord with the tradition and faith of the Church are those official Church documents already cited which call the assembly to grace-filled "actions, gestures and bodily attitudes," call the celebrant to movement signs "performed in such a way that the full meaning and impact shine forth in clear and compelling fashion,"[6] and call for an art of dance "done by truly competent persons in the manner that benefits the total liturgical action."

✨ 9 ✨

The Stillness in the Dance

I n a book entitled *The Liturgy as Dance and the Liturgical Dancer*, the topic of stillness deserves a separate chapter. Otherwise, it might become lost. Because a thing is known most profoundly when known in relation to its opposite, we must embrace liturgical stillness in order to fully appreciate liturgical movement. Article 30 of the *Constitution on the Sacred Liturgy* states: "To promote active participation, the people should be encouraged to take part by means of acclamations, responses, psalmody, antiphons, and songs, as well as by actions, gestures, and bodily attitudes. And at the proper times all should observe a reverent silence." The opposite of acclamations, responses, psalmody, antiphons, and songs is silence. The opposite of actions, gestures, and bodily attitudes is stillness. The full intent of article 30 would seem to be clearer if the final sentence read "And at the proper times all should observe a reverent silence *and stillness*."

There are two opposing fears related to stillness in the liturgy. One is that stillness may be antithetical to the nature of public worship as celebration. Those with this fear like to keep things moving, to keep people from retreating into private prayer. The other fear, for those who treasure times of stillness, is that a renewal of attention to the actions, gestures, and bodily attitudes of ministers and people may signal an end to those precious moments in the liturgy. In my own work, I have encountered both these fears. Once, when planning a liturgy with a priest, I requested several separate moments of stillness within the service. His objection? "We don't want any dead spots in the Mass." While teaching in Australia, I received a rather chilly reception from an Anglican priest in whose Church I was to speak. Following the liturgy, over a cup of tea in the manse, his attitude was remarkably changed. "I thought that because you are a dancer, you would tell us we had to move, move, move all the time. I had no idea you would speak to us also of stillness."

Both the *General Instruction on the New Roman Missal* and the *Directory for Masses with Children* indicate times for silence: after the invitations to prayer, after the homily, and following Communion. These moments, in order to be fully embraced, need to take place in stillness.

Each ministry contributes its own movement to The Dance. Ministers, in the moments they are not actively ministering, need to embrace stillness in order not to divert attention from those who are ministering. While a parish liturgist, I made for our priests a stole with tassels on the ends. At one of the Masses, the celebrant sat and spun the tassels throughout the first and second readings. If I had collected a nickle from every person who said to me, "I didn't hear the readings today, I was too fascinated watching Father spin his tassels," I would have taken in quite a few nickles!

Although not defined in the rubrics, a moment of stillness just before liturgy begins would be helpful. All have been moving—perhaps frantically—throughout the week. Now the community gathers to move together to the Father through Jesus. But before persons can join one another in The Dance, they need to join the scattered pieces of their individual selves. I well understand the resistance of those who have depended on the Sunday Mass for their time to calm down and collect themselves, who are now being asked to jump up and be actively involved with one another. I sympathize with those who have found in the liturgy their one weekly opportunity to be left alone to pray who can't quite deal with their leaders' exhortations to "be aware of the person on your right and the person on your left." It would be wonderful if people could arrive at church calmed and centered, ready to gather heart and hand with those around them. But if they can't, they can be assisted, once they arrive, to gather the scattered parts of their individual selves in order that they might gather with one another. This can be done by beginning the liturgy with one or two full minutes of stillness during which time the ushers would seat no one, and the choir and folk group would stop tuning instruments and arranging papers. At first the stillness might need to be guided. After a while, comment might be necessary only occasionally for the benefits of newcomers and visitors.

No special training is needed to lead a congregation to stillness. The shorter and simpler the instruction, the better. "Close your eyes . . . let go of your tension . . . relax your hands . . . your shoulders . . . your jaw . . . your mind . . . your heart . . . be still . . . " may be all that a congregation needs. Led into a healing stillness for the benefit of their fragmented selves, people will more willingly be led to one another in community worship. Who might be responsible for bringing a community to stillness? Perhaps the very same person responsible for bringing that community to movement! Liturgical dance artists need to be sensitive to moments in their dancing when stillness may speak as powerfully as movement.

The heart of the matter is that both movement and stillness are necessary. We need to move toward God spiritually, physically, emotionally, and mentally; and we need to still the body, spirit, mind, and emotions, and to know that God moves toward us, moves in us, and ultimately, moves us.

✻ 10 ✻

Rhythm and Ritual

The heartbeat of the liturgy as Dance, and of any Christian liturgical dance, is rhythm, the alternation of movement and stillness, sound and silence, action and contemplation. Active participation by means of actions, gestures, and bodily attitudes is vital, but becomes meaningless if it does not alternate with participation through stillness and silence. Special processions or meditations by a dance artist may enrich the Dance on days of great joy or deep penance, but their power would soon pale if performed every Sunday of the Church year. In this chapter, we will treat three different rhythmic polarities as they apply to the art of worship and the art of movement.

Traditional and New

The evensong booklet at Coventry Cathedral says, "You are coming in on a conversation which began long before you were born and will continue long after you are dead."[1] We could say something similar to persons approaching The Dance. "You are coming in on a Dance which began long before you were born and will continue long after you are dead." The question of traditional *or* new gesture in the liturgy becomes meaningless when considered in this frame. We enter the Dance at this moment. But we enter a Dance which reaches, both backward and forward, far beyond this moment and far beyond ourselves. Our dance—the dance of celebrant, member of the assembly, or movement artist—must be shaped by *its* movement. A certain objectivity is required. To throw out movements which do not turn us on today is perhaps to throw out movements which we need today.

One example is the movement of bowing. We in the Western world no longer bow to our betters. Equality of persons means we may stand erect in the presence of all others. The Church calls us all priestly people and enjoins us to practice our faith as mature persons. Bowing the head or the upper body is a sign of humility and submission, of giving up the control that adults are supposed to claim. Yet humble, submissive, and childlike is exactly what we must be before God! A priest once told me that he no longer uses the invitation before the Prayer over the People of "Bow your heads and pray for God's blessing" because "the people don't bow their heads." When I was invited to give the homilies in his church one weekend, I talked to the people about the meaning of traditional movement and prompted them to bow at Father's invitation at the end of Mass. Following Mass, several people told me that the movement of bowing had felt uncomfortable and had been impossible. Others expressed gratitude for the opportunity to move in a way they had often wished to move, but from which they had refrained because people around them had remained standing straight.

I will never forget, at the conclusion of a workshop I was teaching, asking the pastor if he would like to bow while his people prayed God's blessing over *him*. "I sure would!" he said as he sank to his knees and bowed all the way to the floor.

We need both to explore the language of movement for new gestures and movements which speak to us today, and to explore our heritage for movements which link us to the Dance of the ages. Liturgical dancers would do well to found their dances in both new and creative ways of moving and in the ritual movement natural to their faith communities. A ritual gesture, heavy with the weight of tradition, and performed with great artistry, can be the foundation for a powerful Christian dance.

Expressive and Impressive

Some persons complain at the kiss of Peace, "I do not *feel* like embracing my neighbor with a smile, a handshake, or a word of peace." Yet it is not a spontaneous burst of feeling which is called for here, but a conformation of our mind and action to the mind and action of the Church. Mark Searle, director of the Notre Dame Center for Pastoral Liturgy, says it well when he says that the kiss of peace is not "meant so much to be [a] spontaneous reaction to the here and now as [a] disciplined [approach] to the Always and Everywhere."[2] This disciplined approach does not prevent feelings of lovingkindness from arising. It may in fact cause them to arise. But to insist on the feeling prior to offering the gesture is to overemphasize the expressive nature of movement and overlook its impressive nature.

The movement of the priest-celebrant, member of the assembly, or dance artist, may at times arise out of spontaneous feeling or may at times be prescribed by rubric or by assignment. Prescribed movements do not stand in the way of our expressing feeling. They may actually—if we give all our heart and all our bones to them—open up nuances of feeling and understanding which we would never discover if left solely to our own inspiration. We must, however, give our heart as well as our bones to the movement. Knowledge of the power of movement to impress its meaning upon us does not excuse our going through the motions of a Eucharistic prayer or a liturgical dance with no willing involvement.

I am currently working on a dance for which I have been

asked to simply make the sign of the cross during each chorus of the accompanying song. Working on this single movement, made only once during the singing of each chorus, has put me in touch with the very height, depth, and breadth of the cross in relation to my own being, and with the elements of force, time, and design I might call upon to present the sign in the dance.

Repeated and One Time Only

We live in a throw-away culture. A thing used once is discarded. A thing done once is not repeated. As a parish liturgist, I was often guilty of creating throw-away banners and throw-away liturgies. As a dancer, I have often driven myself to keep creating new dances, convinced that no community can bear to witness any dance more than once. We need and appreciate newness because life is continually new. Yet to shun repetition is to deprive ourselves of opportunities to plumb the depths of ourselves, of the liturgy, of life itself.

While doing research for this book, I attended an Antiochian Rite Orthodox liturgy for several weeks. Because I was squeezing that liturgy into an already busy Sunday, I was at first annoyed with the seemingly endless repetitions of word and gesture and the long time everything was taking. After a while, however, I noticed that my annoyance was passing, that I was letting go of the tensions I had brought with me, that I was being borne along by the rhythms of the liturgy. It had taken a long time, and the invitation to join The Dance had had to be repeated over and over again before I heard and accepted it. But it wore down my defenses at last, and I found myself dancing, one foot squarely on the earth, the other unmistakably treading heaven. In the weeks that ensued, I still dashed into the church only an instant before liturgy was to begin (despite intentions to arrange to do otherwise), and the same thing happened. Over and over again. A dance which I have done in the Good Friday liturgy for three years now is highly repetitive. Walking, gently swinging a smoking censor, I precede the cross into the church prior to the Veneration of the Cross. Accompanied by a chant which repeats over and over again "Adoramus Te Domine," I walk, stop, turn, bow, rise, turn, and walk, over and over again. When the large cross is set upright in the church, I continue the movement, but now around the cross: walk, stop, bow, rise, and walk again, each time in a slightly different way but always in the same order. At the conclusion of this movement, the priests join me and, one after another, we kneel, bend in adoration, kiss the cross, and rise. After each one has adored, we bow together and go to our respective places. The people come to adore. Of all the dances I have ever created, of all the technically complicated, interesting nonrepetitive dances I have ever made, this is the dance that reduces people to tears. The reasons are probably many. But one fact remains. The dance is simply a movement of adoration, repeated over and over again, accompanied by a chant of adoration repeated over and over again.

✠ 11 ✠

No Other Single Factor

When the gestures are done by the presiding minister, they can either engage the entire assembly and bring them into an even greater unity, or if done poorly, they can isolate.

Environment and Art in Catholic Worship, art. 56

No other single factor affects the liturgy as much as the attitude, style and bearing of the celebrant.

Music in Catholic Worship, art. 21

The Rev. J. O'Connell's book, *The Celebration of the Mass*, written in 1940, defines the celebrant's movement in the most minute detail. The author presents a long list of "faults in liturgical gesture" which might be committed by the celebrant during the liturgy, and indicates the prayer (*Obscuro te*) which must be said following Mass, on bended knee, to obtain pardon "for defects and faults committed through human frailty in the celebration of Mass."[1]

It is no longer possible or desirable that priests deal with that detailed degree of instruction in rubric. As I teach workshops for clergy and liturgical commissions around the country, however, I discover that the past concern with rubric has not been replaced by training in life-giving ritual movement. With few exceptions, seminaries do not offer training in actions, gestures, and bodily attitudes along with training in homiletics. A priest-friend said to me recently, "The seminary taught us how to preach, but didn't teach us how to move. I guess they figured we would just learn that as we went along." Many young men, ill equipped to *evoke* the spirit of the liturgy in their attitude, style and bearing, resort to *explaining* the spirit of the liturgy, often killing the spirit with words.

Some older men with whom I work plead, "Please don't teach us movements. We had enough of that in the past." The younger men ask, "Please teach us how to move. We want our actions to be as meaningful as our words." The difference in the two requests is subtle, but important. Placed side by side they become "Please don't teach us movements. Teach us how to move." The Rev. J. O'Connell may be passé, but there is a void.

Rules are not needed. Principles are, principles which will enable celebrants to move in ways which help their own prayer and help the prayer of those assembled before them. Let us consider four principles of movement, and then look at several of the actual movements which the celebrant makes during the liturgy.

Knowledge

A thorough study of the *Sacramentary*, the *General Instruction on the Roman Missal*, the *Constitution on the Sacred Liturgy* and the liturgical documents which have followed is in order. Clear directives on movement are given, not in the measured legalistic language of the past but in language which invites the celebrant to awareness of his action in relation to the persons assembled with him in prayer. For example, at the beginning of the entrance rite, "The priest, facing the people, extends his hands and greets all present."[2] The exact form of that movement is dictated, not by legalistic measure but by the "all present" who may comprise a group of fifteen persons gathered in a small chapel for daily Eucharist or a congregation of 500 or more, some of whom may be seated in a distant balcony.

Practice

Liturgical movement "remains an art like any other art, the art of the controlled movement of the body; to be learned by the same work and rehearsal by which any art is learned."[3] Rehearsal does not hinder spontaneity. It provides security, allows for the pruning away of all that is superfluous, and paves the way for powerful yet self-forgetful movement.

The Rev. Leon Cartmell, a marvelous Episcopal cleric and friend whose vision of the liturgy as Dance has often nourished and sustained my own, has this to say about practice:

> Engage in actual, disciplined, instructed practice. We accept as a matter of course, and give considerable attention to the bride's procession . . . no matter how many times we have gone through the same thing. Even the ushers want to know how to escort guests to their seats—and the proper procedure of seating the bride's mother. There are books on etiquette and columns in the papers on the courtesies and amenities of all our conduct in society. Is our Blessed Lord of less importance to us than our neighbors? We are so careful to pay attention to what they might say—but don't seem to give a hoot about how it might appear to the Lord above all forever.[4]

Presence and Transparency

These two principles need to be treated together because at first glance they might seem to be antithetical. How can a celebrant be both present and transparent? In a time when we are urged to "be present" to one another, who wants to be transparent, invisible to others?

The crux of the matter is that the celebrant of the liturgy is called not so much to be present to others as he prays as to be present to the prayer which he prays along with and in the midst of those others. Avoidance of overly individualistic and particularly stylized movement may not indicate an unwillingness or inability to be present, to be true to one's self. It may simply indicate a willingness to be transparent, to enable a congregation to see beyond the celebrant to Christ in all that takes place. Presence and transparency belong together. They are two aspects of a single reality present in the celebrant who can exclaim "Look here!" and then not block the view.

The *General Instruction on the Roman Missal* outlines the movements of the celebrant at the Eucharistic liturgy. A close look at specific movements will be helpful here:

Bowing
Article 84 reads "At the altar the priests and ministers make a low bow." Article 234 reads

> There are two kinds of bows, a bow of the head and a bow of the body:
>
> a) A bow of the head is made when the three Divine Persons are named together and at the name of Jesus, Mary, and the saint in whose honor Mass is celebrated.
>
> b) A bow of the body is made before the altar, if the blessed sacrament is not present; at the prayers: Almighty God, cleanse, and: Lord God, we ask you to receive; in the profession of faith at the words: By the power of the Holy Spirit; in the Roman canon at the words: Almighty God, we pray.... The priest, moreover, bows slightly when he says the words of the Lord at the consecration.

The movement of bowing, and the words which accompany it, should be practiced until the celebrant discovers a unity of the two. That unity may even include moments of silence when the words are complete but the movement continues to its natural end, or moments of stillness when the final position of the movement is held as the words come to their conclusion. Neither words nor movements should be hurried. The integrity of both must be respected.

Sign of the Cross

After the entrance song, the priest and the people make the sign of the cross, a magnificent Christian dance of faith. Later in the liturgy, the celebrant makes the sign of the cross over the Gospel book, over the gifts on the altar, and over the people. This sign, a combination of vertical and horizontal movement, reflects the polarities of transcendence and immanence, of humanity and divinity. Occurring as it does at both the beginning and end of Mass, it embraces The Dance which is both Jesus' praise of the Father and the daily bread of the assembly. The sign, when made on the body or over the assembly, must be "broad and full,"[5] must both express and impress the truth that the whole of each person, and the whole community, is embraced and redeemed. No small or shriveled sign will do when it is our very height and depth and breadth which has been restored. When the sign of the cross is made on persons with oil or ashes, it should be made deliberately and clearly even if that lengthens the procession for oil or ashes by a moment or two.

The Eucharistic Prayer

The celebrant's movement during the Eucharistic prayer would benefit from practice without its accompanying words, enabling the celebrant to familiarize himself with the integrated and organic flow of one movement into another. For example, the following words of the *epiclesis* from Eucharistic Prayer II are accompanied by directions for movement:

Lord, you are holy indeed,
the fountain of all holiness.
Let your Spirit come upon these gifts to make them holy,
so that they may become for us
the body and blood of our Lord, Jesus Christ.

When I am working with priests, I suggest they practice the movement for the *epiclesis* in the following way:

---

fully extend hands and arms, palms up;
slowly raise hands and arms to slightly above shoulder height;
bring hands together, palms facing down, and lower them over
    gifts;
join palms, and bring joined hands back to body;
move right hand out, make clear and deliberate sign of cross
    over gifts;
bring right hand back to join left, and bow.

The movements should be practiced over and over again in silence, allowing the celebrant to discover the integrity that comes when they begin to flow, one movement after another, into a single phrase. Later, when the words are added, both words and gestures can be enunciated with rhythmic integrity.

---

fully extend hands and arms, palms up	to the Lord who is *holy indeed*
slowly raise hands and arms to slightly above shoulder height	receiving from *the fountain of all holiness*
bring hands together, palms facing down, and lower them over gifts	that the Spirit might *come upon* them
join palms, and bring joined hands back to body	on the words *so that they may become for us*

move right hand out, make hands back to body	*the body and blood of our Lord*
bring right hand back to join left, and bow at the name of	*Jesus Christ*

Prayer over the People

We spoke earlier of one congregation's reluctance to accept their priest's invitation of "bow your heads and pray for God's blessing." We did not speak of the priest's movement as he prays the blessing which follows. The foreword to the Sacramentary says "this gesture of stretching his hands over the people is different from the usual extension of hands in blessing. It should be done carefully so that it truly signifies the priest's role as he invokes God's power and strength on the assembly." No exact description of the gesture is given. But there are clues. It needs to be a *strong* movement. Like the movement of greeting at the beginning of Mass, it should give the feeling of God's blessing reaching over the *entire* congregation.

Because instructions for movement in the new rite are given, not in measured legalistic language but in words like the above, they require more attentive study and practice than ever before. If the priest is relieved from the worry of committing faults in movement, he faces the challenge of doing the very best he can.

The Preface Dialogue

The Preface dialogue at the beginning of the Eucharistic prayer is a dialogue between priest and people. The time for the celebrant to find the proper preface in the Sacramentary is before the dialogue begins. To be looking through the Sacramentary while at the same time carrying on a conversation with the assembly is a distraction to all. Article 108 of the *General Instruction on the New Roman Missal* describes the celebrant's movement during the Preface dialogue. In the next chapter, on the movement of the assembly, I have outlined a way in which the celebrant and assembly, already dialoguing verbally while the priest alone moves, can dialogue in both word and movement.

Movements which are not prescribed might be called for out of seasonal or pastoral need. In the parish where I worked as liturgist, we began a custom during penitential seasons which has now become familiar community ritual. At the conclusion of the entrance hymn, the procession stops at the foot of the altar. After the sign of the cross and a few words of introduction, the ministers kneel at the edge of the sanctuary. The people kneel at their pews. Following a minute or two of stillness and silence, the cantor or choir begins a Kyrie. All join. At the conclusion of the Kyrie, all rise, and the ministers go to their places for the opening prayer.

Knowledge of the rubrics for movement in the new *Roman Missal*, the directions they give and the sensitivity they invite, will pave the way for powerful yet self-forgetful celebrational movement. A priest-celebrant's desire to be present to his community in its prayer, and at the same time transparent to that prayer, will nourish movement which captures the attention of the congregation and then directs that attention to God alone.

The two statements from the American bishops with which this chapter began are strong ones. That they bear sober reflection is illustrated by a true story. Several summers ago, I was teaching in a renewal program for priests. One day, the homilist reflected on the movement experiences being offered that week. He said, "Last night I was sitting on my bed wondering if all this movement work Carolyn is giving us is really going to help me or my parishoners. I wondered if I would go home, laugh it off, and forget it. Then I remembered that when I was a boy, there was a priest who genuflected with great care at the Consecration. And I thought about the impression his genuflection made upon me. It impressed me that the man really believed! Now, here I am a priest. When I go back to my parish, I will remember to genuflect reverently because some day there might be a young person in my congregation. . . ."

※ 12 ※

One Body in Christ

Have mercy on this people, which bowed down adore your Godhead. Keep them whole, and stamp upon their hearts the posture of their bodies for the inheritance and possession of good things to come.[1]

A s we consider the actions, gestures, and bodily attitudes of the assembly, it will be evident that although some movements may best be led or taught by the celebrant, some will more appropriately be directed by a movement artist or liturgical dance minister. The formation and training of the latter will be treated in a later chapter. Here we will pause to consider three "scenes" in which celebrant and movement artist might cooperate to facilitate the movement-prayer of the assembly. The scenes are not fictional, but come directly out of this author's experience. Scene One is a homily and post-Communion announcement, Scene Two an hour-long workshop for the parish family, and Scene Three a liturgy into which learnings of the previous week's homily and workshop might be incorporated.

SCENE ONE: *A Homily*

As Catholic Christians, we are a sacramental people. We give—or are given—outward and visible signs of inward and invisible realities of our faith. We know what it is to link outer form and inner meaning. And for good reason. Each one of us was created a unity of outer form and inner meaning, an integrity of body, mind, spirit, and emotions, spirit enfleshed. In the course of time, that integrity was destroyed by sin, and divisions occurred both within ourselves and between us and our Creator. So God became a human person, Spirit Incarnate, to restore all that the Father had created. Jesus did not stretch out his arms on the cross to bring back to the Father just a part of us, only our soul. He did so to save the *whole* of us to the "last shred and fibre" of our being.[2]

For this reason, the Church has always invited to liturgical prayer our physical as well as our spiritual selves: our sense of sight with candles and stained glass, architecture and the visual arts; our sense of hearing with music and the spoken word; our sense of smell with incense, perfumed oil, and flowers; our sense of touch through the various anointings with oil, laying on of hands, and sprinklings with blessed water; and our sense of taste in Jesus' gift of himself as bread to eat and wine to drink. And the Church has involved us in liturgical prayer through our sense of movement and invited us to participate in liturgical prayer in the language of movement, in prayerful action and gesture.

Scripture is full of invitations to know God, and to worship him, in movement. Psalm 95 says, "Come, let us bow down in worship; let us kneel before the Lord who made us." We bow or kneel to express our adoration. Our movement speaks to God. We also bow or kneel in order to know who we are before "the Lord who made us." Our movement speaks to us of God.

Psalm 63:5b says, "Lifting up my hands, I will call upon your name." This ancient gesture allows us to express feelings of praise or supplication, and it stamps upon our hearts the posture of our bodies.

In the tenth chapter of Daniel, an angel of the Lord says to Daniel, fallen on his face in fear, "Stand up, for my mission is now to you." We stand to hear the Gospel, Jesus' words of mission to us. We stand because, from that position, we can move quickly to obey. Our standing can witness to our attentiveness and remind us that we must be ready to serve.

In Sirach 50, we hear that in adoration of Israel's God, and in preparation to receive God's blessing, the people fell prostrate to the ground. A moment when this action still takes place in our liturgy is the entrance rite of the Good Friday service. The priests prostrate themselves before the altar. Wouldn't it be wonderful if some Good Friday we could take all the pews away for that moment, and join our priests in flat-out adoration of the Lord?

The early Church Fathers spoke often of using actions and gestures in prayer, and even of dancing to honor God. Later in Christian history, bodily movement was looked upon with less favor; and for a long time the Church lost sight of the beauty of the whole and integrated person moving in adoration before God. However, recent Church documents from Rome and from the American bishops reflect a renewed awareness of the integrity of the person, and recommend bodily movement in prayer. These documents point to the Church's tradition of movement-prayer, and call for full and conscious participation in the liturgy by means of actions, gestures and bodily attitudes. An entire section of *Environment and Art in Catholic Worship*, entitled "The Arts and the Body Language of Liturgy," invites ministers and worshipers alike to perform their "common movements" of prayer with "uncommon sensitivity."[3]

Let us look for a moment, with uncommon sensitivity, at three common movements we make while praying the liturgy. First, the *sign of the cross*. As we make this sign (homilist make sign as following words are spoken), we trace upon ourselves the very height . . . and depth . . . and breadth . . . of the power of Jesus' redeeming cross in our lives, and acknowledge that by his cross (homilist bring palms of hands together) Jesus has embraced and redeemed us to the last shred and fiber of our being (homilist bow slightly).

Bowing is a movement which we are asked to make every time we say the Creed, at the words "by the power of the Holy Spirit he was born of the Virgin Mary, and became man." To bow, as to genuflect or to kneel, is to lower ourselves, to allow our posture to say to God, "Thou art the great God."[4] Today, at the end of Mass, Father will say, "Bow your heads and pray for God's blessing." I would invite you to bow your head and heart and whole being, and to remain in the bowed posture as Father prays over you the words of blessing. I would also invite you to be aware of whether receiving the blessing in this posture enables you to hear the words in a way that you might not were you to remain standing upright.

Finally, the *sign of Peace.* Tertullian declared that this gesture was the seal of prayer, and that no liturgy was complete without it. He encouraged worshipers to give and receive the sign in such a way that *they create charity.* The sign of Peace in our liturgy today is no mere social amenity, but a sacramental sign that prepares us to approach the table of the Lord in unity.

Let us end now by praying together, with uncommon sensitivity, the sign of our faith (if possible, the homilist should turn and face, with the people, a cross or crucifix while saying, slowly and deliberately):

> In the name of the Father
> and of the Son
> and of the Holy Spirit.
> Amen.

Post-Communion Announcement

This afternoon, at 2:30 in the Parish Hall, Carolyn will lead an informal hour of movement expression for all in the parish family. Wear comfortable, old clothes. Come ready to move, to have fun, and to pray.

SCENE TWO: *A Parish Workshop*[5]

Let us gather here in the center of the room . . . and sit down on the floor . . . if there is anyone who should not sit on the floor, bring a chair over and join us. . . . Good afternoon. I am glad to see you all. What we are going to do this afternoon is relax, and have a good time with each other and with God. Just one request. If I ask you to do something that isn't good for you to do today, feel free to sit out that experience and to come back in on the next.

Do you remember what I said this morning, that you have a movement sense? It is called the kinesthetic sense. Close your eyes . . . put one hand and arm out in front of you, and then slowly raise your hand and arm up over your head . . . and slowly lower your hand and your arm . . . and open your eyes. . . . How did you know it was your hand and arm that were moving, and not your foot? How did you know that you were moving your arm up and down, and not out to the side? Your kinesthetic sense told you! You did not see or hear or touch or taste or smell the movement. You felt it. It is that sense, which tells you that you are moving and how you are moving, that we are going to awaken this afternoon. Are you ready? If you are able to take off your shoes, it will help your movement. I mopped the floor to make sure it was clean for you.

Let us scatter in the room, giving everyone an equal amount of space, filling up all the space, even the space here in the

middle. . . . Let us make some *stretching* movements, movements that have a stretching feeling . . . stretch every part of
you . . . stretch to express and to know that you are awake
and alive on this day of the Lord! . . . Good!

When we come to Church, we say that we are willing to let
go of all the things we are angry or worried about, to let God
have them and let him heal us. As an outward and visible sign
of inward and invisible willingness to let go, *shake* all your
worries out of your hands . . . your arms . . . and (leaning
over) your shoulders. . . . Shake all your worries and angers
out of your head and neck. . . . Stand up, and shake out one
foot and leg . . . the other foot and leg . . . the middle part of
you . . . the whole of you! Shake out your breath and voice
too. Let go!

Sit down for a moment. Sit with your feet out in front of
you and your hands on the floor behind you. . . . Those of
you sitting in chairs can do this, too. Bend your ankles back,
way back . . . now, keeping your ankles back, curl your toes
and the front part of your foot under . . . and keeping your
ankles back and your toes curled, turn the bottoms of your
feet toward one another . . . don't bend your knees . . . this is
just for your feet . . . and let go! Once more, ankles back, toes
under, feet facing each other, let go. . . . You have two arches
in your feet. This exercise strengthens both arches.

Now let us stand up again. . . . Can you bounce? Of course
you can! Bounce on one foot . . . the other foot . . . both feet
. . . bounce on your hands and feet . . . bounce sitting down
. . . lying down. . . . Stand up again . . . and bounce in any
way at all now, but around in the room . . . don't stay in one
place . . . and rest. . . . Often when we've come to church, we
have said or sung, "This is the day the Lord has made; let us
rejoice and be glad in it." Sometimes we sing or say that without any bounce! Let us all bounce together now and say, "This

is the day the Lord has made; let us rejoice and be glad in it."
Each will bounce in his or her own way, but we will all stay
together on the beat. If you meet someone as you are bounc-
ing along, you might proclaim to that person that "This is the
day . . . ." Ready? Here we go. . . . Rest now. Shake your feet
to rest them . . . and your hands, too, if you have been bounc-
ing on them. . . .

Can you *swing* your arms? . . . loosely and freely . . . back
and forth, from side to side, or around . . . let the rest of your
body swing along with your arms . . . don't forget your head
. . . rest a moment. . . . I want to remind you of a story. When
Jesus came to a certain town, he found two sisters. Martha,
who worked very hard to set the table and sweep the floor,
might have made a swinging movement like this (leader swing
with a strong, tight, hard-working feeling). Mary, her sister,
didn't work at all, but sat and listened to Jesus. She might
have made a swinging movement like this (leader make swinging movements that are so relaxed they soon cease altogether).
Our swinging movement today will have some of Mary in it,
and some of Martha in it. It will have lots of letting go, but
enough effort to keep it going. As we swing, we will say over
and over again, "Lórd, we cóme to do your wíll; Lord, we
come to do your will; Lord . . . ."

Can you *open* your hands . . . wide . . . and *close* them . . .
make a fist . . . and open . . . and close . . . open . . . close . . .
can you add your arms, open . . . close . . . and add your head,
open . . . close . . . and your heart and whole being, open . . .
close . . . open, and *stay* open to God who created the sky and
the wind, and the ocean and the birds . . . and now, close, all
the way in, to God who created *you* and lives in you . . . and
once more open, open to God living and present in everyone in
this room . . . open to everyone here . . . and now, when I say
"close," *enclose* at least one other person . . . close! . . . The
peace of the Lord be with you!

When we stand, then kneel, genuflect or bow in church, we are *rising* and *sinking*. For a moment, let us rise and sink freely, discovering what it feels like to sink to the floor, to rise again. Experiment with different ways of rising and sinking. Create new and interesting ways to rise and sink. . . .

Sit down . . . and find a comfortable sitting position . . . close your eyes . . . and begin to *rock* . . . back and forth or side to side . . . move in ways that have a rocking feeling . . . keep your eyes closed if you can. . . . Stop rocking now and open your eyes. . . . All the children come here and sit with me in the center of the room. I am going to read a rocking prayer for the grown-ups. We will be very quiet and still here in the middle while they pray their prayer. I will read the prayer twice, grown-ups. Listen the first time, then pray it in movement as I read it the second time:

> Heaken, O God, to my prayer;
>> turn not away from my pleading;
>> give heed to me, and answer me.
> I rock with grief and am troubled
>> at the voice of the enemy and the
>> clamor of the wicked.
> Fear and trembling come upon me,
>> and I say, "Had I but wings like
>> a dove,
>> I would fly away and be at rest.
> I would hasten to find shelter
>> from the violent storm and the tempest."
>> Psalm 55:2–4a, 6a, 7, 9

Now it is time for the children's rocking prayer. Grown-ups, you sit in a large circle, while the children and I scatter just a bit here in the center. Children, I will read your words twice also. Listen the first time. Then begin your rocking prayer.

> Listen to me, God.
> Hear my prayer and answer me.
> I rock because I am sad and afraid.
> Hold me, God.
> Hold me and rock me
>   until I am not sad or afraid anymore.[6]

Here is a movement everyone can do together, and it is just for fun. *Rolling*. Roll in every possible way ... try not to bump! ....

Stand up.... We are going to *skip* ... everyone in the same direction ... don't worry, grown-ups, you haven't forgotten how ... I'll give you a beat (pace should be lively, and comfortable for adults and children alike) "skip, skip, skip...." Good, let us go in the other direction. Say the word "skip" with me this time.... Now, everyone skip and say something about skipping as you skip. Don't think about what you are going to say. Just start skipping, and the words will come.... Now, begin skipping again, and *say something about God!* .... Good. Sit down and rest for a moment. What were some of the things you were saying? .... Let's make a big circle, and say together Mr. Henry's skip-chant, "Now I know God loves to dance." Bounce in your knees, clap softly on the beat and say "Now I know God loves to dance".... We will keep the chant going while each one who wants to, skips inside the circle. When everyone has skipped who would like to, we will let the chant quiet down....

Sit down ... lie down ... we are going to *relax*. Lie on your back ... with your arms out to the side, palms up, elbows slightly bent, both legs on the floor (not crossed one over the other) ... let your eyes be lightly closed ... your breathing relaxed ... relax your stomach, forehead, your jaw ... think about the feeling of relaxation, of looseness, stillness.... We have been moving a lot. Now we are still. Sometimes it is good to move, and sometimes it is good to be still. At times God speaks to us in such a way that unless we are still we cannot hear him. Just as it is good to move and speak and sing in church, it is good also to be still and quiet, and to sense God moving and speaking in us. (The leader should let the stillness continue in silence for a moment before going on.)

Come to a sitting position now. We will conclude with two things which we can teach the whole congregation some time.

The sign of the cross. While we make the sign of the cross, I will pray some words which will help us with the feeling.

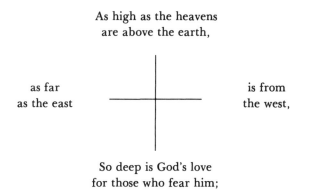

As high as the heavens
are above the earth,

as far   is from
as the east   the west,

So deep is God's love
for those who fear him;

(*open both hands while saying*)
        so far does he reach to embrace
        those who put their trust in him;

(*place palms together and bow while saying*)
        Blessed be the name of the Lord.

The sign of the cross, although most frequently associated with Roman Catholics, seems to be a meaningful dance of faith with many Protestant groups. I have taught it to laypersons, clergy, and seminarians of many Christian denomi-

nations. Several months ago, I was teaching for a United
Church of Christ group. At one of the breaks, a gentleman
came to me and asked "Aren't you going to teach us the sign
of the cross?"

Stand up now . . . and arrange yourselves as if in pews . . .
leave a center aisle . . . I will stand in front so you can all see.
Stand with your feet apart, but not stepping on your neighbor's toes . . . and, with me, rock from side . . . to side . . .
(since the leader is facing the group, he or she will rock to the
right when the group rocks to the left) together as one body . . .
it helps to bend your knees a little as you rock . . . look around
and see that we are all moving as one body. . . . We will take
four rocking beats to raise our hands and arms overhead . . .
then continue rocking while clapping four times overhead . . .
lower your arms on the next four beats . . . and clap in front
of yourself four times . . . then join hands and continue rocking as one united body. . . . We will sing a song now that we
all know, the St. Louis Jesuits' "Sing a New Song,"[7] and we
will move together as we sing.

Sing a new song unto the Lord;	slowly raise hands and arms until all the way over head
let your sóng be súng from moúntains hígh.	clap overhead, on the syllables accented opposite
Sing a new song unto the Lord, singing ál - le - lú - iá. ´	slowly lower hands and arms clap on accented syllables
(during verses)	take hands with those to left and to right, and everyone rock together

When the above is done in church, those in the procession
move in unison with the people during the chorus, but they

move forward up the aisle rather than in place. As each verse begins, the procession stops moving forward and the ministers take hands to the left and to the right with members of the congregation. All rock together throughout the singing of the verses. Each time the chorus repeats, the procession resumes its forward movement toward the sanctuary. The above song is simply an example. Each community will have a song with which it is familiar. The parish movement artist can create simple congregational movement for that song.

SCENE THREE: *A Liturgy*

What follows is a listing of movement prayers that might be used in the liturgy. Some are traditional, others new and creative but built on the traditional. The latter should never be taught as substitutes for the former, but as experiences to deepen involvement in liturgical prayer and deepen understanding of the movement heritage of the Church. One would not use all the following experiences on a single Sunday. Some experiences might be taught by the celebrant, some by the movement artist. Some need leadership only as long as necessary to acquaint or reacquaint the congregation with a particular gesture. Others might require a leader each time they are done.

At one church here in Tucson, the celebrant comes out before Mass to invite the congregation's "uncommon sensitivity" to one of the movement prayers to be emphasized that day. If it is a penitential season, the form might be kneeling or beating the breast at the Confiteor. If in the Gospel the congregation is to hear Jesus' call for unity, it might be the sign of Peace or holding hands at the Our Father. The parish movement artist might also be called upon to encourage or demonstrate the movement-prayer to be emphasized that day.

The possibilities for the *Entrance Procession* and *Sign of the Cross* have already been described in this chapter.

The Confiteor

The only place in the liturgy where the movement of striking the breast is retained in the rubric is on the words "in my thoughts and in my words" of the Confiteor. If, as hoped by Romano Guardini, the gesture is to be valuable as a hammering against the fortresses of the heart in order to open them to grace, "an honest blow, not an elegant gesture," it needs some renewed attention. A fist placed squarely over the heart has power. The gesture should be more than the mere flicking of the fingertips.

Kyrie

Sung in Latin or in English, the Kyrie might be prayed in movement as follows:

Lord have mercy	While singing *Lord have mercy*, celebrant or deacon brings both closed fists to breast, palms toward body, and bows head slightly; holds position while people repeat words and movement. People then hold this position as leader continues.
Christ have mercy	Leader, singing *Christ have mercy*, opens hands and arms, and lifts head; holds position as assembly repeats. People then hold their final position as leader continues.
Lord have mercy	Leader, singing *Lord have mercy*, returns to first, closed

position; holds position while
people repeat. People remain in
final bowed position as celebrant stands erect, opens his
hands and arms toward them,
and prays.

*May Almighty God have mercy
on us, forgive us our sins, and
bring us to everlasting life.*

The Readings

The readings are from God's Word which seeks to move into
us and to move us. Whatever lector or movement leader can
do to enable the congregation to cease its own movement and
come to a relaxed stillness will facilitate the hearing of the
Word. This assistance can be given verbally or by example.
Because of the integrity of the whole human person, a closed
posture with arms and legs tightly crossed is not as good for
receiving the Word as a posture which is open, both feet on
the floor, spine erect, hands open in lap.

The Psalm

The people might be led in a simple, mantra-like movement
as they chant, or even recite rhythmically, the psalm anti-
phon. They would then hold the final position of their movement while the cantor or lector presents each verse. Since
many psalms were originally written to accompany movement, this seems a natural way to pray them.

Alleluia

An Alleluia chant before the Gospel which contains six Alle-
luias (I have used the melody of Jacques Berthier's "Bene-

dicte Domino"[8]) allows the use of a series of movements which are reminiscent of both Eastern practice and of the familiar three-fold signing with the cross on forehead, mouth, and heart.

Alleluia	place palms together, thumbs touching chest, and bow slightly
Alleluia	move joined hands to lips, and raise head
Alleluia	move joined hands to forehead
Alleluia	open hands upward, and reach toward Gospel book
Alleluia	slowly lower hands, arms remaining outstretched
Alleluia	bend elbows, place palms together, thumbs touching chest

When the Gospel book is held by a book bearer, the celebrant can join his congregation in the movement which greets Jesus' Word.

The Creed
All bow at the words "by the power of the Holy Spirit he was born of the Virgin Mary, and became man."

Preface Dialogue and Sanctus

The Lord be with you.	celebrant extends hands and arms to greet all present
And also with you.	members of congregation extend hands and arms to greet celebrant

Lift up your hearts.	celebrant raises hands and arms well overhead, with clarity and power
We lift them up to the Lord.	congregation repeats celebrant's movement
Let us give thanks to the Lord our God.	celebrant joins palms together overhead, then slowly and clearly lowers them to a position chest-high
It is right to give him thanks and praise.	congregation repeats celebrant's movement

On the word, "Holy, holy, holy," all bow. On the words, "Hosanna in the highest," all rise from bow.

The Communion Procession

The Communion hymn should be such that the people need not carry books with them nor even have to read music projected on a wall. To walk with others in procession is a sacramental act, a dance of unity, and it deserves attention. A sung mantra like those from Taizé elicits congregational participation in the Communion song without diverting visual attention to anything other than the community moving together to the table of the Lord.

Receiving Communion

Like the swinging movement, the movement of receiving Communion raises the question of Mary and Martha. "Martha" actively reaches out to take the Host in hand. "Mary" passively opens herself to be fed. Both are valid, and are simply two sides of one coin. There is sign value in all communicants receiving in like manner. Yet to disparage one way of receiving while encouraging the other is to fail to recognize that people's spiritualities are different, and that any one individual may choose to receive in different ways on different occasions. Communion in the hand, recently restored to the liturgy, is often problematic, however, because it is not well done. A wholehearted reaching out with open or crossed hands[9] is quite a different matter from snatching the Body of the Lord with one's fingers. Pausing briefly to the side of the Eucharistic minister to communicate one's self is a different matter altogether than eating on the run. Communion in the hand is potentially a powerful gesture. But it needs to be taught, again and again if necessary, as carefully and prayerfully as any of the other power-filled movements of The Dance.

13

Christian Folk Dances

Because I believe so strongly that dance as a language of prayer and celebration belongs to everyone, I spend as much time enabling others to dance as I do sharing my own dances. Until very recently, I felt that many sacred dancers in this country were in the mind-set of "let us dance, and let the people watch." I believe that is changing. On a recent East Coast and Midwest tour I met many persons who told me that the communities they belonged to were beginning to dance together. That is a wonderful and healthy thing. Dance artists who know and love the language of movement and who wish to share the beauty of that language, should challenge themselves to discover (and if they cannot discover, to create) simple Christian folk dances which they can teach to their communities. Margaret Fisk Taylor, in her book *A Time to Dance*, relates a comment made by the Rev. William F. Lynch, S.J., on "The Catholic Hour" television program on January 20, 1963. It could well be applied to the topic of this chapter.

> We propose that you come out among us in America and either find us or help us find ourselves. . . . You must send your real artists out among us and we will work together. At first we will be shy and difficult, but the human greatness will come out of us and we will teach you what real movement and style is.[1]

Teaching the people (the folk) to dance is as much a part of a dance ministry as is dancing for them. The Church is of that understanding now in music, and efforts to teach the folk to sing are bearing fruit. We need to know and teach the same in the art of movement, that art which calls the whole person to involvement in worship.

Church picnics, retreats, pot-luck suppers, prayer meetings, Sunday School classes, even business meetings offer times when the informal fellowship provided by folk dances can be beneficial. A simple folk dance can relax minds and bodies, break down barriers of communication, ease concerns for rank and importance, welcome newcomers to an established group, encourage a spirit of cooperation, prepare the way for a congregation to worship together as a unified body. Circle and line dances, the most basic group dance forms, can be easily performed by anywhere from a half-dozen to several hundred people.

A NEW COMMANDMENT

I learned this song while I was teaching in Australia in 1982. I wanted to teach a Christian folk dance to the group with which I was working, but found that they did not know my songs. I asked, "Sing me something you all know," and they sang this song. The movement, which was made up on the spot, is simple and possible for even the most beginning groups.

I would teach the movement for this dance, then the song, and finally put the two together.

(*Preparation*)

Stand in a circle holding hands. Turn to face right, ready to step on right foot.

Take eight steps, starting with right foot. On the eighth step, pivot around, and then take eight steps, starting with right foot. On the eighth step, face center.

Take two steps in, two steps out, two steps in, two steps out. On the two steps in, swing joined hands and head upward, and the two steps out, swing joined hands downward and backward, and bow head slightly.

Repeat the entire dance, adding at the end of the repeat: Clap hands and open them to greet all in circle, then immediately make one full turn to the left in place and return to starting position.

KING OF KINGS AND LORD OF LORDS

A friend of mine was singing at a Christian coffee house one evening. As she sang this song, I saw in my imagination a dance which could be done either in one circle or in concentric circles. The singing and dancing could be in unison or, if in concentric circles, as a round. The following week, my liturgical dance group, Romans XII, learned it. The following month, we taught it to the audience at our biannual concert.

During the first half of the dance, all are standing in circle, facing center, elbows bent, palms facing outward and joined to palms of those on either side. During the second half of the dance, all are facing left, palms touching palms of those on either side.

First half:

King of kings and   step sideward right with right foot, then bring left to meet right

Lord of lords   step right with right foot, then bring left to right

Glory	clap hands, and open quickly overhead
Alleluia	bring hands slowly down to starting position

Repeat first half, then turn immediately to face left in preparation for second half.
Second half:

Jesus	step left
Prince of Peace	step right
Glory	step left while at the same time clapping and opening quickly hands overhead
Alleluia	step right, while at the same time slowly returning hands to joined position

Repeat second half. If the group is in two or more concentric circles, the dance can be done in a round. The second group begins the first half when the first group begins the second half.

Variations on the second half:

1) Clap *after* "Glory," but *before* "Alleluia." When the dance is done as a round, the clap of the group doing the second half will happen slightly after the clap of the group doing the first half.

2) Still clapping after "Glory," but before "Alleluia," allow the clap to cause a hop. Do not change feet on the hop.

BEHOLD HOW GOOD

Behold How Good (Hine Ma Tov) is a traditional Israeli folk song. I have changed the words slightly. The dance, which I have reworked over a period of time, may vary from the traditional. There are many folk songs and dances from the Jewish and other nations which would be enjoyable for church communities. I have learned several deeply Christian dances from a friend who is a Sufi. Usually, I teach the song *Behold How Good* first. Then I teach the dance.

Before learning the dance, practice two group positions.

Position 1:   stand in lines of three or four, *side by side*, hands resting on each other's shoulders

Position 2:   Starting in Position 1, each person make a quarter turn to the right, leaving right hand where it is, transferring left hand to own left shoulder

---

The dance begins in Position 2.

Take four steps forward, beginning on right foot, followed by eight (twice as fast) steps forward beginning on right foot. Repeat.

Quickly change to Position 1,
    and step sideward to the right on the right foot,
    bring left foot to meet right;
    step forward on right foot,
    bring left to meet it;
    step sideward to the right on right foot,
    bring left to meet it;
    step backward on right,
    bring left to meet it.
    Repeat.

❧ 14 ❧

The Facets of Ministry

T he dancer who works to facilitate the community's participation in The Dance through ritual and creative gesture and folk dance, may also serve that community by occasionally sharing a well-crafted dance offering. In the same way, a trained soloist or choir ministers both by leading the assembly's song and by offering a gift of song for the assembly to hear. The question is, should the artist dance for the congregation before leading it in its own movement, or should the communal movement come first? When the question is asked about music, the answer seems clear. Church teaching is that the congregation's song is first in importance. Theoretically, the same is true for the art of movement. The actions, gestures, and bodily attitudes of the assembly and its ordinary ministers are primary. But theory is not always possibility. At times, I am asked to dance for the people before being allowed to either work with them or speak to them. In those instances, I feel it important that I choose dances which are simple enough that the people can feel them along with me even though they themselves are not moving.

One of the more successful dances in these situations is the one in which I dance with a lighted censor, accompanied by chant and wearing a long, habit-like dress. The dance, the song (either in Latin or English), and the garb link past and present, familiar and new, tradition and a contemporary shaping of that tradition. The movement is extremely simple. Specialized dance movements which isolate me as dancer from the congregation simply will not do. Later, when the people's kinesthetic sense is awakened, and when the congregation is aware that it, along with the dancer, can pray in the language of movement, such simplicity, although always desirable and wonderful, is not as imperative.

At what moments in the liturgy are contributions by the dance artist appropriate? Let me answer by sharing some actual experiences.

The Entrance Rite

A Lenten dance by the Romans XII liturgical dance group, which I founded and directed for four years, began with a silent procession led by dancers and followed by servers, lector, and celebrant. When all reached the sanctuary, ministers went to their accustomed places, dancers to their starting positions scattered throughout the sanctuary. The movement which followed was penitential in nature, accompanied by selected lines from the Gospel of the day and the sounds of cymbal and drum. It concluded with an *a capella Kyrie eleison*, sung antiphonally by dance group and congregation. The opening oration of the day followed.

A Reading

One Ash Wednesday, I was asked to dance the Isaiah 58 reading. I accompanied myself, speaking the memorized reading as I danced. On other occasions, I have danced that same Scripture while the lector has read. When the dancer speaks the reading there is a built-in integrity of word and movement. Practice is required for the unity of the lector's word and the dancer's movement. If the dancer moves in front of or near the lectern, the congregation's focus need be in only one direction to follow the Word.

The Psalm

Occasionally I will ask a congregation to pray the day's psalm with me as follows:

antiphon	congregation and I sing the antiphon while moving together (people remain seated; I am usually standing in order to be visible to all);
	we end the movement in a position which can be comfortably held during the verses.
verses	I dance the verses while the congregation remains in the final position of the antiphon;
	at the end of each verse, I rejoin the congregation for the repetition of the antiphon

The Gospel Acclamation

During a workshop, I will often ask participants to dance with their Bibles, first in silence, then while singing an *Alleluia,* and finally while processing and singing *Alleluia.* Results are often exquisite, dancers holding the Word of God aloft, sometimes open, sometimes closed, bowing with the book, showing the book to the left and to the right. Whenever an individual's creation seems particularly beautiful or appropriate, I invite that dancer to present the book at the following day's liturgy. He or she will dance with the book during the *Alleluia,* present it to the one who will read, and hold it during the reading, uniting for that moment the ministries of dance artist and book bearer.

Memories of two such Gospel processions come to mind.

One was created by a 76-year-old nun at the Rochester Franciscan Motherhouse in Rochester, Minnesota, the other by a teenage boy in Australia. The first was marked by a beatific smile on Sister's face as she danced and by her joyful exclamation after Mass, "I'm a liturgical dancer!" The second elicited awed comment after liturgy that "He moved with the book as if it really meant something to him. It made me want to listen."

Presentation of the Gifts

The time of the preparation of the altar and the presentation of the gifts is a low moment in the rhythm of the liturgy and needs to be respected as such. A grand offertory procession is not in accord with liturgical structure. However, I recently witnessed the New Genesis Sacred Dancers from Our Lady of Perpetual Help Church in Glendale, Arizona, dance a solemn but extremely simple presentation and preparation. Their walking, turning, lifting and presenting the gifts, and their setting of the table, had about it a quiet, domestic reverence which knitted the liturgy of the Word to the liturgy of the Eucharist. It was so in accord with the structure of the liturgy that it was transparent.

Communion Meditation

Following Communion is an excellent time for a nonverbal reflection on all the words which preceded in the day's celebration. I have created many dances for this time in the liturgy. If no definite theme is given, my favorite dances for post-Communion meditation are either of two dances with English handbells, one of which is described in the chapter "A Variety of Gifts." The sound of the bells is beautiful, and the total unity of sound and movement required to dance and ring the bells simultaneously is healing, both to do and to behold.

A word about the *Our Father*. Mysteriously, some liturgical dancers and dance groups, looking for something to dance, gravitate toward the Lord's Prayer. The problem with that is that the Our Father belongs to the assembly, not to a soloist or small group. Accepting the argument that a prayerful dancing of the Our Father may enable a congregation to pray with the dancers vicariously, it seems to me unwise to ask the assembly to pray the Our Father vicariously at all, since there are other and better moments for dance in the liturgy. When the Lord's Prayer is to be danced, it seems fitting that it be danced by all, led by the dancers.

We have considered three shapes which the liturgical dancer's ministry might take: leading congregational gesture, teaching congregational folk dance, and dancing for the liturgy. There are other possibilities as well: teaching in religious education programs, and assisting acolytes, lectors, ushers, and celebrants with their movements and gesture. In the parish where I was liturgist, the ushers, many of them older gentlemen, were enthusiastic participants in The Dance. Once I asked them to carry flags in procession, to walk, bow, and turn in unison. They practiced hard, did well, and loved their ministerial role. They were always eager to know what their next dance assignment might be!

Another option for the liturgical dancer's ministry is forming and directing a group of persons who wish to work regularly on dance as a language of prayer. In the fall of 1978, I offered a class in sacred dance and opened it to all interested persons in Tucson. Because the purpose of the class was not to prepare things to be shown, but simply to dance together prayerfully, people came who never would have come had they thought their work was going to be seen. Three months after the class began, we had an invitation to dance for an evening liturgy. Not a single person in the group hesitated to accept. While some laughingly accused me of knowing all along that we might be invited to dance publicly, they accepted the invitation because they wanted to share what they did on Wednesday nights.

The weekly classes of Romans XII[1] continued, almost without interruption, twelve months a year, for four years. Participants ranged in age from nine to seventy, and the group ranged in size from a half-dozen to over twenty. Although we danced in numerous liturgies and eventually gave concerts (which always included dances for the audiences as well), the main focus of the group was simply the Wednesday night prayer-and dance-time together. Because I am on the road so much these days, Romans XII is on sabbatical. But I have no doubt that it will resume again in the not-too-distant future.

Where does the person who wants to grow in the varied aspects of a dance ministry begin? Where does one get education and experience? First, there is no substitute for praying for the vision that is right for one's particular situation. Subsequently, training need be sought in both liturgy and dance. Several centers which offer courses in liturgy and the arts, and in liturgical dance, are listed at the back of this book. Dancers should take advantage of liturgy congresses and of liturgy workshops offered at religious education congresses in their own or any nearby diocese. There are excellent written resources on liturgical movement and dance. The bibliography of this book lists many. Finally, a dancer might encourage the local liturgy committee or diocesan commission to enlist the services of a trained liturgical dance artist and teacher for a short-term study program.

❧ 15 ❧

Professional Prayer?

Often I am asked if liturgical dancers, who wish their dancing to be prayer, need pay attention to education, discipline, and craftsmanship. Do not such things stand in the way of prayer? The question has many sides and must not be answered carelessly. The American bishops set standards for the arts which are to serve the liturgy, and perhaps it would be good to begin our discussion of the question with the bishops' standards. The following are from *Environment and Art in Catholic Worship*.

> Quality means love and care in the making of something, honesty and genuineness with any materials used, and the artist's special gift in producing a harmonious whole, a well-crafted work. This applies to music, architecture, sculpture, painting, pottery making, furniture making, as well as to dance, mime or drama—in other words, to any art form that might be employed in the liturgical environment or action (Art. 20).

> Processions and interpretations through bodily movement (dance) can become meaningful parts of the liturgical celebration if done by truly competent persons in the manner that benefits the total liturgical action (Art. 59).

> The work of art must . . . be capable of bearing the weight of mystery, awe, reverence and wonder which the litur-

gical action expresses; [and] it must clearly *serve* (and
not interrupt) ritual action which has its own structure,
rhythm and movement (Art. 21).

... A kind of transparency [is demanded], so that we
see and experience both the work of art and something
beyond it (Art. 22).

These are demanding standards. They demand that the dance
be well-crafted, of genuine material, "capable of bearing the
weight of mystery, awe, reverence and wonder," and offered
by dance artists who are "truly competent" and liturgically
sensitive.

When we speak of "truly competent" artists, we inevitably
raise questions of experience, training, discipline, technique,
even professionalism. Questions such as these, far from being
contradictory to the work of the liturgical dance artist, are
helpful, even necessary, to it. Prayer itself is a discipline, one
which requires continuous practice and which benefits from
the training and guidance of a wise spiritual director. Training, discipline, and technique must indeed be taken seriously
by the liturgical dancer; but, because of the artificiality and
affectation attached to these words in the conventional dance
world, some effort to redefine them is in order.

The bishops have made it clear that there can be no pre-
tentiousness, no artificiality, in the arts used in the liturgy.
The liturgical dancer's movement technique must be *natural*
and "genuine." It cannot consist of patterns and positions
which are contrary to the God-given structure of the human
body and its ways of moving. A well-known dancer stated on
national television recently that "the essence of choreography
is to make the body do that for which it was not designed, and
yet make it appear natural."[1] There is no place for thinking
like this in liturgical dance.

Because the God of whom the liturgical dance will speak is limitless, the dancer's movement vocabulary must be one which is continuously expanding, never a limited, closed system of "dance movements." A unique, never-been-created-before child of God, each dancer has the capacity to explore and reveal the things of God in ways that have never been created before, to continuously discover new material, new ways to move. I have been accused of being undisciplined in my work because, instead of relying on nameable patterns of movement, I am always in search of just the right movement to bear a particular feeling or meaning. Far from being easy or undisciplined, the search is a soul-rending, body-aching discipline that never ends. Were it not for the satisfaction and relief that come from finally discovering just the right movement, I would flee to another discipline in an instant.

Along with the work in "genuine" movement and the creative search for meaning-filled movement, the liturgical dancer must study any traditional movement which might exist in his or her practice of the faith. By knowing the language of The Dance of his or her tradition, the artist can build on that tradition both pastorally and creatively.

The liturgical dancer must learn to trust his or her kinesthetic sense, relying on what is revealed through inner feeling during the movement work rather than on outward appearance. The dancer must let the kinesthetic sense lead, and allow the other senses to take their rightful, secondary, place. This is often helped by working without mirrors. Before I anger many dancers who work frequently with mirrors, let me say that there are times when mirrors are helpful. Once a dance is created, checking it in front of a mirror aids in clarifying its visual aspect. A mirror, however, can stand in the way of a dancer's kinesthetic awareness, and it cannot clarify either the force or the time elements of movement.

A mirror should probably not be used during the first creative efforts of the dance lest the visual sense alone operate and control. The reader may notice that I did not suggest that priests videotape themselves or watch themselves in mirrors. As with the dancer, the mirror or videotape is helpful as a check on the visual element of the movement, but cannot provide for the celebrant's kinesthetic awareness. We live in a visually-orientated society. The visual sense is the most externally-oriented of the senses. The dancer or celebrant wishing to minister in a gathering at which there are no "onlookers," only participants, must learn to awaken and trust the most interior sense, the kinesthetic sense. And if the celebrant or dancer is working kinesthetically, his or her work will be received kinesthetically, communicating far more than the eye can see or the ear can hear.

Along with the disciplines of seeking a natural, continuously expanding, kinesthetically alive language of movement, the liturgical dancer must undertake a discipline of letting go, relaxing, allowing the self to *be moved* by the Spirit. In other words, the dancer must be willing to become an ecstatic. Only God can enable one to "stand outside of" the self in the dance, but the artist must be willing to let go and let God work. Letting go of the self and its appearances is a surprising discipline in an art which places, from the theatrical point of view, a premium on presenting the self and its appearances. There is hard work in the letting go, but the fruits are worth the effort.

The imperatives presented so far in this chapter may sound a bit intimidating to the beginning liturgical dancer or to the parish or diocesan commission struggling to define a vision for liturgical dance. However, these standards apply to simple things: kinesthetic awareness, natural movement, and the abandonment of self.

One word mentioned at the beginning of the chapter still lacks definition: professionalism. Distinctions often made between the professional and the amateur are that one works for money while the other works out of love and interest; one performs the work full time, the other part time, as a hobby; professional work is excellent in quality while amateur work is of poor quality. Our interest here is in the last-mentioned understanding. Judith Rock, a liturgical dancer and author from California, reminds us that the word amateur comes from the Latin word for love. An amateur *loves* what he or she does. It stands to reason that if one truly loves what one does, he or she will do the very best job possible, will not settle for anything of poor quality, especially if it concerns the things of God.

It is the opinion of this author that liturgical dancers must be amateurs who spare no effort of prayer or practice to create high quality work. I have often heard people say that liturgical dance does not need to be as good as dance outside the church. They are only partially right. It does not need to be "as good." It needs to be better. It needs to be so good that "from the greatness and the beauty of created things their original author, by analogy, is seen" (Wis 13:5).

A noted liturgist-musician wrote me once that one of the greatest threats to the acceptance of liturgical dance in this country is amateurism. He did not mean enjoyment and love of dance. He meant shoddy work. Too many well-intentioned dancers take lightly their responsibility to offer excellent work to the liturgy or believe that hard work may interfere with prayer. Just as a celebrant's enthusiasm for spontaneity in his liturgical prayer can never substitute for knowledge and practice of that prayer, so can the dancer's desire to pray never substitute for his or her practice of prayer in the medium of movement. Hard work and thorough preparation, far from standing in the way of prayer, may clear the way for prayer to take place. I am not saying that one should not offer a danced prayer in the liturgy without ten years of daily practice. St. Augustine encourages efforts on all levels of expertise when he says, "Do not allow yourselves to be offended by the imperfect while you strive for the perfect."[2] What I am saying is that when one desires to shape an art work to be offered in the Church's prayer, both love and discipline are required.

A few words about obedience, service, and transparency. Service and obedience are words to which we often attach negative significance today. Yet the liturgical dance artist is called to obedient service to God, to the work being created, to the liturgy, and to the community and those in authority in the community. The artist may feel that he or she has been given a divine mission which must be undertaken with complete artistic freedom. But, within the Church's liturgy, that mission must also be understood as a commission, the artist's need for freedom balanced by the needs of those who request and who will receive the art. To seve is a privilege and, in the words of Madeleine L'Engle, "it is to our shame that we tend to think of it as a burden."[3] My own experience has led me to believe that I can ask for no more exciting or fulfilling role, as an artist of the Church, than that of obedient servant.

Environment and Art in Catholic Worship reminds us that "a certain transparency" is required in those arts and artists who would serve the liturgy. The dancer whose gift would grace the prayer of the Church must, like the celebrant, be able to say "Look here!" and then get out of the way. The challenge to the movement artist is great. Unlike the painter and composer who can remove themselves from the work once it is complete, the movement artist is forever present in the work. Transparency is possible, but it comes only to those who truly desire it.

❧ 16 ❧

Rose Petals and Rocks

L et me now tell you a story. It is the story of one person's
search for and daily work in dance as a language of personal and liturgical prayer. It is my own story.

As a child, I took ballet lessons for several years with Phyllis
Marmein in upstate New York. I also danced alone many
evenings in our living room while my father played his records.
During those evenings, I made up my own movements, danced
from my heart, and possessed some wonderful notion that I
was dancing with God. Although I did not think much then
about wholeness, I now know that those times in the dimly
lighted living room were some of the most integrated moments
of my young life.

At college I majored in religion, took modern dance classes,
and joined the dance club. I remember, my senior year, performing a dance with another religion major, in which he
and I unrolled rolls of toilet paper across the stage, shouting
at the top of our lungs Paul Tillich's theological profundity of
"ultimate concern!" After graduation, I worked as a religious
education director in a Methodist church. On Tuesday afternoons, three junior high school boys met me in church to
work on sacred dance. I did not really know what I was doing,
but I knew it felt right, and the boys kept showing up. At an
evening service that year, the boys showed a dance they had
created.

A year later, I read an announcement for a summer course

in creative dance taught by Barbara Mettler at her studio in
Tucson, Arizona. Not knowing anything about Barbara Mettler or the Tucson Creative Dance Center, but knowing that
my college roommate lived in Tucson and that I would have a
place to live during the summer, I enrolled in the course.
That four-week course brought everything together for me.
Barbara Mettler taught dance as a creative art activity. She
trained us to move in ways that were in accord with natural,
God-given body structure and to dance in cooperation with
the Creator within. She taught us to move as individuals,
each one different and beautiful, and to move as a cooperative
group, each individual contributing to the life of the common dance.

We improvised freely, grew in awareness of our movement,
shaped and controlled what we had become aware of, sometimes composing dances out of the material that had revealed
itself during the time of work in freedom and awareness. Then
we began again in freedom. Over and over again. Although
Barbara had created her center as a laboratory in pure creative dance, and did not teach dance as an expression of any
one faith or creed, I knew instinctively that I was again dancing with God. There was no way of discerning, during those
four weeks, the amount of work, discovery, discipline, pain,
and joy which lay ahead in this way of work. But I discerned
enough to return to New York, resign my job, and pack the
car for the long drive back to Tucson.

For three and a half years, I took all the classes Barbara offered while working full time as her assistant, which in those
days meant secretary, cleaner, summer course organizer, and
errand girl, eventually teaching children's and adult classes
of my own. It was during this time that I found my way into
the Catholic Church and its Dance.

I married, and after a while my husband's work took us

back to upstate New York for a year and a half. While there I taught creative and sacred dance for churches, YWCAs, camps, conferences, a preschool, a community college, and everywhere else I could find a receptive group. Upon our return to Tucson, I took a job as a religion and creative movement teacher in our parish school, and when the school moved to another location, remained with the parish as full-time liturgist for four years. I danced alone every day in the parish hall next door to my office.

These days, I work independently, traveling throughout this country and Australia, lecturing, teaching, and dancing. I am grateful that Barbara Mettler still allows me the use of her studio and that the parish still allows its ex-liturgist the use of its parish hall for daily work.

Each dance artist enjoys a daily discipline which is uniquely his or her own. I cannot say what the way of work of another artist will be. I can, however, describe my own and hope that it might be nourishing and encouraging to others. The daily work begins with relaxation. Lying on the floor, I relax the body, checking to see where there is tension, letting it go. I also relax the mind and the emotions, letting go of conscious worries and concerns. These things I know are not lost. They are simply liberated to surprise me in fascinating, even healing, ways in the dancing that will follow. I also relax the spirit. I am aware of my spiritual poverty, my unfaithfulness to prayer, my unworthiness to dance in the Lord's name, but rather than grit my teeth over all of that, I prefer to open myself to the possibility of prayer now as I dance.

Relaxed, I begin to move, stretching, twisting, bending, moving in ways that awaken and enliven my movement feeling. I work each part of the body separately, experimenting, exploring—and at the same time strengthening—the movement of every part. Work with my breath and voice is included at this time. Then I move the whole body again, but from place to place, walking, skipping, crawling, rolling, leaping, running, and moving throughout the space, up in the air and down on the floor in ways that are not even nameable. After resting for a moment, I begin my "dance for the day." Totally improvised, it is created out of seeming nothingness yet is deeply rooted in the something of who I am and what my needs and feelings are at that moment.

If I improvise long enough, I can marvel at the wondrous fact that, without my mind willing my muscles to do so, I move in a wide variety of ways. I discover myself moving in ways I could never have planned in advance. If I move slowly or forcelessly, in curves or on a regular beat for a while, I soon find I am also moving fast, forcefully, in straight lines, and with wonderful irregularities of beat. Although the dance is hard work, there is also a sense that it is a work done through me, requiring only my willingness to be danced.

Because the use of recorded music might prevent the discovery of inner rhythms and qualities, this initial work is done in silence except for the occasional sounds of my own breath, voice, hands, or feet. In creating a dance for a liturgy or concert, I will often create both the dance and its sound accompaniment, speaking, singing, or playing a musical instrument while I dance. This process I find exciting because it allows me to create a unity of sound and movement. Several of these dances and their accompaniments are described in the next chapter. On other occasions, I dance to music composed and performed by friends. When I do work with a piece of recorded music, I find it helpful to isolate, and work separately with, beat pattern, melody, quality of sound, and lyrics if any.

As the reader may surmise, this way of work requires that a dancer work alone regularly and often. Even when I have been working with others, either as director or member of a dance company, I have sought time to dance alone every day. I cannot imagine wanting to be a religious dancer and not desiring dance time alone with the Creator. I noticed, while directing my liturgical dance company, that those who worked alone had consistently more to offer to the group.

The daily discipline is not easy. I am still amused by those who, unaware of the constantly dirty feet, aching bones, and sweaty practice clothes, believe that all the liturgical dancer does is waft blissfully about. A couple of years ago I complained to my spiritual director about the loneliness, the hard work, and the frightening dry times which seemed to follow every creative peak. His reply shook me then and does even now. "Did you expect that this path you have chosen would be strewn with rose petals? Let me tell you, baby, there are rocks in the road, and the best of us go on our hands and our knees, bleeding."

The struggle to continually grow in competence as a Church artist *is* worth it. There are rocks in the road, but there are rose petals along the way, too. Much work is required, but it is work only to reveal the grace, beauty, and meaning which God has already placed within. My task is simply to weave my way among the rocks, dig up the soft earth below, weed, water, cultivate, and occasionally, always in God's time, to bloom.

⚘ 17 ⚘

A Variety of Gifts

In those occasional times, in God's time, when the blooms appear, what are they? What is the nature of the dances that emerge? What are they about? The dances are as varied in nature as life itself. They are inevitably "about" something deeply important to me, whether or not I was aware of that importance before the creation of the dance. Each dance is a gift gratefully received. Each is, in a sense, greater or better than I the dancer am. Madeleine L'Engle speaks words familiar to many an artist when she says, "I believe that each work of art, whether it is a work of great genius, or something very small, comes to the artist and says, 'Here I am. Enflesh me. Give birth to me.' And the artist either says 'My soul doth magnify the Lord,' and willingly becomes the bearer of the work, or refuses; but the obedient response is not necessarily a conscious one, and not everyone has the humble, courageous obedience of Mary."[1]

It is with gratitude now that I magnify the Lord for the gifts he has bestowed, even for the pain I have known in giving birth to each one. Some of the dances came out of an assignment. Others were simply created with no particular usefulness in mind. I did not know if the latter would ever be seen, and that never seemed to matter. Looking back now, I realize that each dance which reached maturity was shared, and that each reached maturity just as it was needed.

True Fasting

This dance began as an assignment, and provided the first occasion for me to speak an extended portion of Scripture as I danced. Created ten years ago, the dance even now continues to grow and change. The creation of the *True Fasting* dance first involved memorizing Isaiah 58:4b-12,14, then experimenting to discover movements which expressed different words, phrases, and sections. I then began to speak the Scripture as I danced, seeking a unity of the rhythm of the words and the rhythm of the very abstract movements which has evolved out of my work with those words. Then I critiqued the dance. Were there different degrees of force used in the dancing of "false accusation" and the dancing of "watered garden," different time elements felt in "lie in sackcloth and ashes" and "ride on the height of the earth"? Was there variety in the design element, or true presentation of the emotional content? Were there places where stillness would speak? Was the dance a unified, organic whole, not just a series of interesting movements strung together? Creation and critique alternated with each other (they cannot operate simultaneously in me without one blocking the other), until I knew in my heart that the dance was finished, for the time being.

True Fasting was first shared as a reading for Ash Wednesday liturgy. Since then it has been offered as a reading for penance services and for a city-wide ecumenical Thanksgiving service. It is also used as a concert piece. Dancing the verses of Isaiah 58 has planted those words of Scripture deep within me. There is something about memorizing a portion of Scripture and then declaring it with one's whole being that knits it into the fabric of one's life. There is a mysterious thing about *True Fasting* and the other Scripture dances which I do. I cannot now sit still and recite the text without effort, but when all my bones are involved in praying the text, the words flow out as if of their own accord.

The Bell Dances

These dances have been delightful gifts. I was asked by a music publisher to create dances to music for English handbells. Knowing nothing about handbells, I joined the bell choir at a local Congregational church. Although I stayed with the bell choir for six months, I knew, the first time I put a bell in my hand, that I was not interested in creating dances to bell music. I wanted to dance with the bells! A member of the choir had bells of her own and had the courage to lend me the four bells I needed to work on *Peace Is Flowing Like a River.* (Now, owning my own bells, I am awed by her courage.) That dance was shared first at a handbell festival, but has since been offered many times as a post-Communion meditation in churches.

The second bell dance, an *Alleluia* with three variations, took several months to create. They were months of anguish. Carrying four handbells while one dances is not as easy as turning on a recording of music. Because the ringing of any one bell causes a movement, it was important to discover which order of holding the bells elicited the kind of movement I was looking for. Should the E and the F sharp be in one hand, the G sharp and A in the other? Or should it be E and A, G sharp and F sharp? F sharp and A, E and G sharp? The possibilities were seemingly endless and each one had to be tried. Finally, one combination was settled upon, and the work began. It went well at first, but when roadblocks appeared the bells were put away for a week or so, and other dances were worked on. The *Alleluia* bell dance required several periods of work and rest from work before its final form emerged. It was not an easy birth, yet the dance that eventually came forth was deceptively clean and simple. *Alleluia* is most frequently offered as part of an entrance procession or as a meditation after Communion.

Daniel 3

Daniel 3 (verses 57–90 in the New American Bible) began, like *True Fasting,* as a dance to be self-accompanied by speech. It has been performed that way on one occasion, but it is normally accompanied by a reader from the church or organization for which I am dancing. The excitement of this dance for me, since every reader proclaims the Scripture differently, lies in creating a unity of movement and sound. The basic structure of the dance remains always the same, but its elements of force and time are blown apart and re-created with each new reader. The dance covers a lot of space, and so with each new environment must be redesigned to accommodate altar rails, steps, and aisles. *Daniel 3* is offered as a reading or a prayer of praise. The dance grew out of a conversation with my spiritual director. I was feeling depressed. He suggested I go hiking, look at the beauty along the path, and thank God for each beautiful thing I saw. He predicted that the thanksgivings would gather momentum and lift my spirit. He was right. It seemed that every rock, flower, and breeze was alive with God. The next time I came across the Daniel passage in Lauds, I knew I would dance it.

The Mary Dances

I said earlier in this chapter that my dances are "about" things which are important to me whether or not I am aware of their importance when I begin work on them. As a convert to Catholicism fifteen years ago, Catholic attention to Mary was uncomfortable for me. For years, try as I did to understand, my discomfort continued. Then I began to dance about Mary, and the Lord began to teach me about her. By dancing *The Reed* (I taped my own reading of Caryll Houselander's poem against the sound of an unaccompanied bamboo flute), I learned of Mary's emptiness, her willingness to surrender and be filled. By dancing the *Magnificat*, composed and performed by my friend Chris Yirka, I learned of her joy and her strength. By dancing *The Bride*, accompanied by John Michael Talbot's music, I learned of her spirit of contemplation and her spirit of celebration. The Lord's ways are truly mysterious and marvelous. I now have created more dances on Marian themes than on any other single theme! The Mary dances are usually presented during Advent, before the Gospel or as part of the homily.

Veni, Veni Emmanuel

This is a very simple dance performed with a lighted candle and accompanied by the *a capella* chanting of "O Come, O Come Emmanuel" in either English or Latin, either plainchant or metered song. The accompanist usually comes from the community for which I am dancing, so the dance changes subtly each time it is offered. *Veni, Veni Emmanuel* can be used in many ways. It can be danced in the aisle, leading the entrance procession to the sanctuary. It can begin in the aisle and continue in the sanctuary after other participants in the procession have reached their places. It can be danced as a pre-liturgy gathering or centering prayer, or as a meditation between readings. If danced at the beginning of the liturgy, the dancer could conclude by lighting the candles of the Advent wreath. If danced before the Gospel, the dancer might stop in front of the pulpit, raise the candle, and remain standing motionless during the Gospel reading.

Cindy's Dance

While teaching religion and creative movement in our parish school, I tried to relate the movement classes to the liturgy of the day or season. As Holy Week approached one year, I created a dance for the children in which I was Judas, a child was Jesus, and the other children were mourners, moving in unison in small groups with leaders, and finally carrying Jesus away. It was a simple dance, but during the dance Jesus had to stand with his arms raised unsupported *for a long time.* Seven-year-old Cindy was Jesus. Cindy's mother telephoned me to say that Cindy was practicing holding up her arms at home, and that her arms were hurting her. I quickly told Cindy she didn't have to practice holding her arms up, and if her arms hurt, we could ask someone else to be Jesus. No, she informed me. She wanted to be Jesus, and if her arms hurt, that was all right because Jesus' arms had hurt, too. We shared the dance at school. It was well received, and we were asked by the parish to share it just before the Veneration of the Cross at Good Friday liturgy. At the end of that liturgy, as we were preparing to leave, I glanced toward the large wall crucifix now lying on the sanctuary steps, and stopped, stunned. Cindy was sitting cross-legged on the floor at Jesus' head, rubbing his arms and comforting him. Several years later, members of Romans XII re-created this same dance for Good Friday. They did well, but I know in my heart the dance will always be, for me and for all who witnessed it that first night, Cindy's dance.

Are the dances just described creative or ritual dances? I would submit that they are both. All have resulted from reaching deep into interior creative resources, and all have been, from their conception, knitted to the liturgy which I so love, and to its needs.

Who am I to dance at liturgy? Who am I to discover and develop dances which can serve the liturgy? No one. That is just the point. The dances are gifts. It is all gift.

❧ 18 ❧

Unless You Become...

The development of gestures, postures, and actions is very important for Masses with children in view of the nature of the liturgy as an activity of the entire [person] and in view of the psychology of children.

Directory of Masses for Children, art. 33

The principles of active and conscious participation are in a sense even more valid for Masses celebrated with children. Every effort should be made to increase this participation and to make it more intense.

Directory of Masses for Children, art. 22

Much depends not only on the actions of the priest, but also on the manner in which the children conduct themselves as a community.

Directory of Masses for Children, art. 33

Two years ago, I was asked to teach a workshop entitled *Liturgies for Little Ones* at our diocesan religious education congress. I began by defining "little ones" in two ways: the *chronos* definition of four-to-twelve years of age indicated on the congress brochure, and the *kairos* definition which calls all Christian believers "little ones." That is not to say that I ignored the congress committee's assignment, but I did try, at the outset of the workshop, to lift participants out of the mindset that liturgies for little ones are Masses for the kiddies to celebrate while we adults watch.

Liturgies for little ones are, rather, Masses for children to celebrate *with* adults who love them and who wish to lead them "toward the celebration of [those] Masses in which the Christian community comes together on Sundays."[1] When the adults who plan liturgies for children forget the above, the result may be childish rather than childlike. The danger in childish children's liturgies is that little ones, when it is time to "put away childish things" (1 Cor 13:11), may put away Sunday liturgy altogether.

If we believe that gestures, postures, and actions are "very important . . . in view of the psychology of children" but forget that they are "very important . . . in view of the nature of the liturgy as an activity of the entire [person]," we risk reducing liturgical movement expression in children's liturgies to fun and games. There is nothing wrong with inviting children to fly like butterflies and swim like fish as they sing in church as long as those actions do not replace or take precedence over the traditional language of the Church, which belongs to young and old alike. This is not the opinion of a stodgy adult, but of children with whom I have worked as a teacher or parish liturgist over the years. The most frequent request I received from children was to teach them the form and meaning of the movements the adults make. The children wanted to learn, to be absorbed into the greater community, to join The Dance.

When invited to work with children, I begin with a basic movement workshop like the one described in the chapter "One Body in Christ." Sensing in their bodies both the naturalness of movement expression and the power of their movement to express and impress feeling, the children are then ready to embrace the dances of the Christian liturgy: the sign of the cross, genuflecting, bowing, moving in the entrance, Gospel, offertory, and Communion procession,[2] and receiving Communion in the hand. They are ready to dance the Preface dialogue with the celebrant, and open their hands and hearts to each other in the greeting of Peace. They do not hesitate to move outwardly as well as inwardly as they sing, even clapping the regular beat of a hymn. They are ready to embrace liturgical stillness.

Many adults with whom I have worked do not believe children are receptive to stillness. I can only relate my own experience. While teaching religion and creative movement in the parish school, I included a short time of stillness in every class. One day, late and unprepared for class because I had had to play the organ unexpectedly for a funeral, I asked the children to give me a few moments to gather my wits and plan a class. "Don't plan a class, Mrs. Deitering," the four-to-nine-year-olds responded. "Let *us* teach today." Every child taught for three minutes. Every child taught something different, based on favorite past experiences in class; but *every* child concluded his or her time with, "Lie down on your back . . . close your eyes . . . breathe . . . relax . . . be still. . . ." I was amazed. I enjoyed the most relaxing class I have ever taken.

At the beginning or conclusion of a liturgy with children, I occasionally teach a simple Christian folk dance, if space allows.

For several years after leaving school teaching, but while still employed by the parish as liturgist, I taught an after-school group called Creative Movement for Young Christians. Occasionally the group would prepare simple processions or dances for the liturgy. One Christmas Eve, the children danced the entrance procession, carrying the infant Jesus, entering the main aisle, encircling the altar, and eventually moving to the Crib to place the Child within. One little fellow who had not rehearsed the dance at all, but who had been in creative movement classes while I taught in the school, joined the procession as it went by. His mother was aghast. "Don't worry, Mom," he said. "I'll just follow the feeling." And he did.

Children are often more capable than are we adults to instinctively understand the power of the movement and to embrace The Dance. We can teach them to a certain degree. But we must also allow them to teach us. Children have taught me to be wide-eyed with wonder at the sign of the cross, to genuflect with care, to "follow the feeling" of a community at prayer, to enjoy being totally involved. The challenge of working with children is two-fold: to be childlike for their sake and to be childlike for our own sake. Only then will all present be able to approach the table of the Lord as children of God.

❧ 19 ❧

One Battle at a Time

> The wearing of ritual vestment by those charged with leadership in a ritual action is an appropriate symbol of their service as well as a helpful aesthetic component of the rite.
>
> *Environment and Art in Catholic Worship*, art. 93

"What do you wear?" is often the first question people ask me upon learning that I am a liturgical dance artist. Although I want to ask in return, "Is that question really of first importance? Wouldn't you rather ask me why I dance, or inquire about movement in liturgical prayer," I recognize that clothing for liturgical dance must be of importance for the question to be asked so often, so soon. The question reflects a major fear concerning dance in the liturgy and a major obstacle to its acceptance. How we "clothe these parts" may either free those hesitant about liturgical dance to accept it or cause them to condemn it.

Because I believe clothing for the dance is an issue secondary to the dance itself, I am willing to dress in a way which eliminates possible stumbling blocks and which frees people to receive the dance. Because I believe that liturgical dancers are "charged with leadership in a ritual action," and that liturgical dance artistry can be both a ritual action and "a helpful aesthetic component of the rite," I feel that garments used for the dance are a kind of vestment and are required to "invite [the same kind of] appropriate attention" that any vestment must. The dance artist is performing a service and a function in the liturgy. Vesture used must draw attention to the service and function without drawing undue attention to the person performing it.

It is not possible to make arbitrary rules about what should or should not be worn as liturgical dance costume-vesture. It is possible, however, to state several principles: The dance is to serve the Body, not the body. Personal reflection on dance costuming needs to be balanced with corporate reflection. Especially when dance is a newly developing ministry in a parish, the dancer needs to listen to the needs (and fears) of the Body and to be obedient to those in authority in the Body. When I am offering a dance in a parish which has not seen dance before, I often wear a long dress with long sleeves. I am in no way trying to be prudish. Rather, I am trying to free people to consider the dance without the question of my clothing blocking that consideration. A person can only fight one battle at a time.

Most of the time I dance barefooted. The "holy ground" on which I dance demands that I, along with Moses, take off my shoes. Because of the variety of floor surfaces in churches, dancing barefooted is also safer than dancing in shoes which do not allow one to feel the floor. However, there are times when I am asked to dance in shoes, and I respect the request. Once, just as a Mass was to begin, I thought I saw a pastor look with some dismay at my bare feet. I asked him if he would feel more comfortable with my dance to present the Gospel book if I wore shoes. He assured me that he would. I ran and got the only shoes I had with me, heavy leather sandals which, by the grace of God, looked fine with my habit-like dress. After Mass, the pastor told me he was delighted with my "reverent" dance. Perhaps the shoes enabled him to see the reverence. Since not all my costumes look good with heavy leather sandals, I now carry several kinds of soft dance shoes with me when I travel.

Today's liturgical dancer is paving the way for the liturgical dancer of the future. What I *want* to wear must be weighed against what I know will keep the door open to a Christian art of dance not just for myself but also for those who will follow me. Dance artists who serve the Church, especially at this time in history, must recognize that they are called to be not just artists, but ministers and educators as well. A friend recently defended a man who had danced at liturgy in tight jazz pants and a tank top, a costume I felt inappropriate. She said, "He is just a dancer, not a crusader like you." I do not believe that anyone can afford to be "just a dancer." Rather, I believe that every liturgical dancer is called to be an artist, minister, educator, humble servant of the prayer of the Church, and crusader as well. Being an obedient servant has never made me feel as if I was compromising my artistic freedom to costume a dance in accord with its content and meaning. Rather, it has enabled me to costume dances in ways which allowed my artistic freedom to function in cooperation with the Church.

The *True Fasting* dance is performed in a long brown dress tied with a heavy rope belt. The bell dances are done in long dresses with very full skirts. The *Daniel 3* dance, which includes many different qualities of movement in many different positions, is presented in a sleeveless jumpsuit which is gathered at the ankles, under which is often worn a bright contrasting blouse or leotard. The Mary dances have been costumed in a variety of ways, usually peasant skirts and blouses, or long dresses.

Every dance is created first, costumed later, enabling the dance to define the costume needs rather than the other way around. Costuming for liturgical dance may be beautiful without being expensive. Many of my costumes have come from second-hand clothing stores and been remade for dance. Others, I or friends have made.

❊ 20 ❊

One Dancer's Vision

O ver twenty years ago, the people of God were called to full and active participation in the liturgy "by means of ... actions, gestures and bodily attitudes."[1] Since then, documents both from Rome and from the American bishops have pleaded for an awareness of the whole person at worship.[2] "Valid tradition reflects ... attention to the whole person." Attention to things such as gesture and movement is "one of the urgent needs of contemporary liturgical renewal."[3]

A document from the American bishops has pointed to the power of the priest-celebrant's movement to unite or isolate a praying community.[4] It has called the assembly to an uncommon sensitivity to their common movements of liturgical prayer.[5] It has offered a tentative invitation to a liturgical art of movement "done by truly competent persons in the manner that benefits the total liturgical action."[6]

Major educational efforts are required to bring the vision of the liturgical documents to life. Future priests must have opportunity to learn not only how to speak, but also how to move with clarity, understanding, and beauty.[7] They must have opportunity to learn how to "promote the liturgical instruction of the faithful, and also their active participation in the liturgy both internally and externally."[8] The people of God must learn that what they outwardly do at liturgy is impressed inwardly, and that the movements they make to express their prayer (and the stillness they embrace in that prayer) can offer them more wholeness than can words or silence alone.

"Major and continuing effort is required . . . to restore respect for competence and expertise in all the arts and a desire for their best use in worship."[9] Movement artists who wish to serve the Church and its Dance must be offered, or must avail themselves of, education to form them as artistically, theologically, liturgically, and pastorally mature ministers.

Long- or short-term study courses at seminaries or through diocesan offices or worship might begin to provide the education which is needed. A center for Christian sacred and liturgical movement, under the auspices of the American Bishops' Committee on the Liturgy, could offer courses for priests and other liturgical ministers, movement artists, religious education directors, teachers, and whole families, teaching the people of God to celebrate with all their heart and all their bones.

One closing thought. We live in complex and critical times. One might question the importance of beautiful celebrational movement, of the movement prayer of the gathered people of God, of the grace-filled artistry of a liturgical dancer. Who is fed, and what wars are averted, by dancing? What political and economic injustices are made right, what misunderstandings and hurts healed by celebrating The Dance with beauty and integrity? An old Jewish tale, the source of which I have long forgotten, gives us a clue.

A learned rabbi was coming from afar to visit a certain town. The town's citizens gathered to await his arrival, and a great din arose as they argued many points of philosophy upon which they disagreed and which they would place before the rabbi to settle for them. When the rabbi arrived and noticed all the bickering he began to hum a tune. Soon all were humming with him. Then the rabbi put words to his tune. Soon all were singing. Finally, he began to dance as he sang. Before long, the entire town was dancing. All were dancing together. When the dance ended, the rabbi bowed politely and said to the townspeople, "I trust I have answered all your questions."

On with the dance. On with The Dance.

Appendix

The liturgical dancer seeking training and education in liturgy will find help by contacting the local liturgical commission or diocesan office of religious education. Also, there are national offices of liturgy and music, such as the National Association for Pastoral Musicians, which often offer work in "the allied arts," such as dance.

For information on regular or occasional courses in liturgical dance, the dancer might contact:

In the United States

The Sacred Dance Guild

President, Susan Cole
3917 N.E. 44th Street
Vancover, WA 98661

Eva Herndon and Joan Sparrow
Membership Director
82 Hillside Drive
Carlisle, MA 01741

Doug Adams, Director
Summer Course in Sacred Dance
Pacific School of Religion
1798 Scenic Avenue
Berkeley, CA 94709

The Rev. Thomas Nankervis, Director
National Clown, Mime, Puppetry and Dance Ministries
Box 24023
Nashville, TN 37202

The Rev. Edd Anthony, O.F.M.
The Brown Bag, West
1229 S. Santee Street
Los Angeles, CA 90015

Bro. Greg Zoltowski, O.F.M.
The Brown Bag, East
Siena College
Loudonville, N.Y. 12211

In addition to the above, there are numerous arts organizations and schools and colleges offering courses in liturgical dance in various parts of the country.

Barbara Mettler's intensive summer course offers a foundation in pure creative dance. Write 3131 N. Cherry Avenue, Tucson, AZ 85719.

In Australia

Mary Jones, Coordinator
Christian Dance Fellowship of Australia
P.O. Box 373
Milson's Point
N.S.W. 2061
Australia

In England

Lola Webb, Editor
Religious Dance
11 Yardley Court
Hemingford Road
Cheam, Surrey
England

Notes

Abbreviations for Church Documents

CSL   *Constitution on the Sacred Liturgy*
EACW   *Environment and Art in Catholic Worship*
MCW   *Music in Catholic Worship*

Chapter 1: The Dance

1. St. Ambrose, "On Repentance," 6:42, as cited by Margaret Fisk Taylor, *A Time to Dance* (Philadelphia: United Church Press 1967), p. 77.
2. *Constitution on the Sacred Liturgy* (Washington, D.C.: United States Catholic Conference Publications Office, 1963), art. 14.
3. *Environment and Art in Catholic Worship* (Washington, D.C.: United States Catholic Conference Publications Office, 1978), art. 56.
4. Ibid., art. 55.
5. Ibid., art. 59.
6. *CSL*, art. 10.
7. Evelyn Underhill, *Worship* (New York: Harper and Row, 1936), p. 33.

Chapter 2: Ritual and Creative Beauty

1. Thomas Pinkel, in Preface to *Actions, Gestures and Bodily Attitudes*, by Carolyn Deitering (Saratoga, Calif.: Resource Publications, 1980).

2. A.K. Coomeraswamy, as cited by Joseph Campbell, *Myths to Live By* (New York: Bantam, 1972), p. 123.
3. Madeleine L'Engle, *Walking on Water: Reflections on Faith and Art* (New York: Bantam, 1982), p. 72.
4. Peter Brooks, "Leaning on the Moment," *Parabola* 4, no. 2 (May 1979): 53.

Chapter 3: Gift and Burden

1. Romano Guardini, *Sacred Signs* (St. Louis: Pio Decimo Press, 1956), p. 14.
2. *EACW*, art. 5.
3. Ibid., art, 35.
4. *Music in Catholic Worship* (Washington, D.C.: Bishops' Committee on the Liturgy, 1972), art. 5.
5. "Whereas other senses inform us of events which occur in the world around us, the sense of movement informs us of events which occur within ourselves. It is that faculty which coordinates the various parts of our bodies and enables us to function as an organized unit" (Barbara Mettler, "The Art of Body Movement," *Ten Articles on Dance* [Tucson: Mettler Studios, 1973]).
6. Timothy Kallistos Ware, "The Transfiguration of the Body," in *Sacrament and Image*, ed. A.M. Allchin (London: Fellowship of St. Alban and St. Sergius, 1967), p. 23.
7. Gerardus van der Leeuw, *Sacred and Profane Beauty: The Holy in Art* (New York: Holt, Rinehart and Winston, 1963), p. 55.
8. *EACW*, art. 4.
9. Cited in Ware, p. 30.

Chapter 4: Sacred Act and Priestly Office

1. Curt Sachs, *World History of the Dance* (New York: W.W. Norton, 1937), p. 4.
2. Maria-Gabriele Wosien, *Sacred Dance: Encounter with the Gods* (New York: Avon Books, Art and Cosmos Series, 1974), p. 13.
3. *EACW*, art. 30.
4. Ibid., art. 59; see also art. 25.

Chapter 5: From Miriam and David

1. Written in Hebrew between 200 and 175 B.C., the book of Sirach was not included in the Jewish Scriptures after the first century A.D. It has always been recognized by the Catholic Church as divinely inspired and canonical.
2. E. Louis Backman, *Religious Dances in the Christian Church and in Popular Medicine* (New York: Greenwood Press, 1977), p. 10; originally published in 1952.
3. W.O.E. Oesterley, *The Sacred Dance* (Cambridge, England: At the University Press, 1923), p. 44f.; see also Constance Fisher, *Dancing the Old Testament* (Austin, Texas: The Sharing Company, 1980), p. 8.
4. W.O.E. Oesterley, "Early Hebrew Ritual Festivals," in *Myth and Ritual*, ed. S.H. Hooke (London: Oxford University Press, 1933), pp. 117–18.
5. Fisher, p. 18; see also Curt Sachs, *World History of Dance*, p. 93 (see chap. 4, n. 1, above).
6. Leon Wood, *The Prophets of Israel* (Grand Rapids: Baker Book House, 1979).
7. Gerardus van der Leeuw, *Sacred and Profane Beauty*, p. 29. (see chap. 3, n. 7 above).

Chapter 6: Bishop Ambrose and Company

1. Tertullian, "On Prayer," chap. 16, *Fathers of the Church* (New York: Fathers of Church, Inc., 1959), vol. 40, p. 172.
2. *History of the Councils of the Church: From the Original Documents*, ed. Chas. Joseph Hefele, D.D. (Edinburgh: T. & T. Clark, 1895), p. 434.
3. Several translators of the Fathers use the phrase "stand on tip-toe." Backman believes such translations to be incorrect. "There are some who translate these little-noticed words by 'rise up on tip-toe,' which seems incorrect, because we shall encounter the words 'move the feet' as a technical term for *dancing*" (*Religious Dances*, p. 22 [see chap. 5, n. 2, above]).
4. St. Augustine, "Commentary on the Lord's Sermon on the

Mount," chap. 5, n. 4, *Fathers of the Church* (New York: Fathers of the Church, Inc., 1951), vol. 11, p. 125.

5. Tertullian, "Apology," chap. 30, *Fathers of the Church* (New York: Fathers of the Church, Inc., 1950), vol. 10, p. 87.

6. Tertullian, "On Prayer," chap. 23, p. 182.

7. Theodore Klauser, *A Short History of the Western Church* (Oxford: Oxford University Press, 1965), pp. 114-15.

8. St. Clement, "Letter to the Corinthians," *Fathers of the Church* (New York: Cima Publishing Company, 1947), vol. 1, p. 32.

9. Tertullian, "On Prayer," chap. 14, p. 170.

10. Ibid., chap. 17, p. 172.

11. Michael Moynahan, S.J., "Embodied Prayer in the Early Church," *Modern Liturgy* 6, no. 5 (August 1979): 25.

12. Moynahan, *Embodied Prayer*, NCR Cassettes (Kansas City: NCR Publishing Company).

13. Ibid.

14. Romano Guardini, *Sacred Signs*, p. 30 (see chap. 3, n. 1, above).

15. St. Augustine, "Sermons" 6:3, *Fathers of the Church*, vol. 11, p. 325.

16. Tertullian, "On Prayer," chap. 18, p. 173.

17. Hélène Lubienska de Lenval, *The Whole Man at Worship* (London: Geoffrey Chapman, 1961), p. 60.

18. As cited by Margaret Fisk Taylor, *A Time to Dance*, p. 75 (see chap. 1, n. 1, above).

19. St. Ambrose, "Letters to Bishops," chap. 28, *Fathers of the Church* (New York: Fathers of the Church, Inc., 1954), vol. 26, p. 145

20. As cited by Backman, p. 20.

21. St. John Chrysostom, as cited by Backman, p. 32.

22. Backman, p. 32.

23. As cited by Backman, p. 31.

24. As cited by Taylor, p. 75.

25. As cited by Backman, p. 32.

26. Backman, p. 49.

27. As cited by Taylor, p. 77.

28. St. Ambrose, as cited by Backman, p. 29.

29. St. Ambrose, "Letters to Bishops," chap. 28, p. 145.

30. St. Gregory of Nyssa, "Ascetical Works: On the Christian Mode of Life," *Fathers of the Church* (Washington, D.C.: Catholic University Press, 1966), vol. 58, p. 154.

31. St. Basil, "Ascetical Works: An Ascetical Discourse," *Fathers of the Church* (New York: Fathers of the Church, Inc., 1950), vol. 9, pp 207–15.

32. St. Augustine, *City of God*, Book XIV chap. 2, *Fathers of the Church* (New York: Fathers of the Church, Inc., 1952), vol. 14, pp. 348–50.

33. St. Augustine, "Faith and Works," chap. 27, *Fathers of the Church* (New York: Fathers of the Church, Inc., 1955), vol. 27, p. 280.

Chapter 7: Full Circle

1. Dom Gregory Dix, *The Shape of the Liturgy* (London: Dacre Press, 1945), p. 15.

2. Ibid., p. 141.

3. D.M. Hope, "The Medieval Western Rites," in *The Study of the Liturgy*, ed. Cheslyn Jones, Geoffrey Wainwright, and Edward Yarnold (London: SPCK, 1978), p. 239.

4. Dix, p. 18.

5. As cited by Margaret Fisk Taylor, *A Time to Dance*, pp. 82–83 (see chap. 1, n. 1, above).

6. As cited by E. Louis Backman, *Religious Dances*, p. 48 (see chap. 5, n. 2, above).

7. Taylor, p. 83.

8. As cited by Backman, p. 78.

9. As cited by Backman, p. 81.

10. Taylor, p. 94.

11. Backman, p. 71.

12. Taylor, p. 92.

13. P.L. Travers, "Walking the Maze at Chartres," *Parabola* 8, no. 1 (January 1983): 23.

14. Backman, pp. 66–73; see also Taylor, pp. 113–14.

15. Backman, p.121.

16. Ibid., p. 48.
17. Taylor, p. 103.
18. As cited by Taylor, pp. 89–90.
19. Backman, p. 155.
20. Ibid., p. 157.
21. Ibid., p. 59.
22. As cited by Taylor, p. 135.
23. Douglass Shand Tucci, "The High Mass as Sacred Dance," *Theology Today* 34, no. 1 (April 1977): 58.
24. Jacques Maritain, *Art and Scholasticism* (New York: Charles Scribner's Sons, 1930), p. 56.
25. Curt Sachs, *World History of the Dance*, pp. 392–93 (see chap. 4, n. 1, above); see also Gerardus van der Leeuw, *Sacred and Profane Beauty*, p. 53 (see chap. 3, n. 7, above).
26. *Noticiae II* (1975), 202–5, as cited by the Bishops' Committee on the Liturgy Newsletter, vol. 18 (Washington, D.C.: National Conference of Catholic Bishops, April/May 1982): 14–16. *Noticiae II* is a semiofficial news release published by the Congregation for the Sacraments and Divine Worship. According to the BCL *Newsletter*, the Congregation termed this statement on dance to be "a qualified and authoritative sketch" and "an authoritative point of reference for every discussion on the matter." The BCL *Newsletter* commended the Congregation's "essay" for study by diocesan liturgical commissions and offices of worship.
27. *CSL*, art. 124; also *EACW*, art. 20.
28. Sachs, p. 4.

Chapter 8: What Do the Documents Say?

1. Josef Jungmann, *Commentary on the Documents of Vatican II* (New York: Herder and Herder, 1966), vol. 1, p. 22.
2. *EACW*, art. 34.
3. *MCW*, art. 20.
4. *CSL*, art. 122.
5. Ibid., arts. 122, 124.
6. *MCW*, art. 7.

Chapter 10: Rhythm and Ritual

1. Erik Routley, "Theology for Church Musicians," *Theology Today* 34, no. 1 (April 1977): 26.
2. Mark Searle, "Liturgical Gestures," *Assembly* 6, no. 3 (December 1979): 80.

Chapter 11: No Other Single Factor

1. Rev. J. O'Connell, *The Celebration of Mass* (Milwaukee: The Bruce Publishing Company, 1940), p. 401.
2. *General Instructions on the New Roman Missal*, art. 86.
3. Ralph Adams Cram, as quoted by Douglass Shand Tucci, "The Hight Mass as Sacred Dance," *Theology Today* 34, no. 1 (April 1977): 69.
4. Rev. Leon Cartmell, in a letter to the author.
5. *EACW*, art. 56.

Chapter 12: One Body in Christ

1. Prayer from an Armenian liturgy, quoted by Michael Moynahan on *Embodied Prayer*, NCR Cassettes (see chap. 6, n. 12, above).
2. Romano Guardini, *Sacred Signs*, p. 14 (see chap. 3, n. 1, above).
3. *EACW*, art. 55.
4. Guardini, p. 20.
5. I am indebted to Barbara Mettler, founder and director of the Tucson Creative Dance Center, for the vision and definition of dance which underlies my workshop teaching.
6. Carolyn Deitering, "You Can Move!," *Rainbows, Dreams and Butterfly Wings* 1, no. 3 (Carthage, IL: Good Apple, Inc., January–February 1983): 25.
7. Dan Schutte, S.J., "Sing a New Song," published by North American Liturgy Resources, 10802 North Twenty-third Avenue, Phoenix AZ 85029, copyright 1972.

8. Jacques Berthier, "Benedicte Domino," published by GIA Publications, Inc., 7404 Mason Avenue, Chicago, IL 60538, copyright © 1978, 1980, 1981, Les Preses de Taizé (France). International Copyright Secured, all rights reserved.

9. "Patristic Teaching," *Body of Christ* (Washington, D.C.: Bishops' Committee on the Liturgy, 1977), pp. 11–13.

Chapter 13: Christian Folk Dances

1. As cited by Taylor, *A Time to Dance*, p. 151 (chap. 1, n. 1, above).

Chapter 14: The Facets of Ministry

1. "And now, brothers, I beg you through the mercy of God to offer your bodies as a living sacrifice holy and acceptable to God, your spiritual worship. Do not conform yourselves to this age but be transformed by the renewal of your mind, so that you may judge what is God's will, what is good, pleasing and perfect" (Rom 12:1–2).

Chapter 15: Professional Prayer?

1. Alexander Gudonov, in interview on PBS television, 2 March 1983.

2. As cited in *MCW*, art. 27.

3. Madeleine L'Engle, *Walking on Water*, p. 23 (see chap. 2, n. 3, above).

Chapter 17: A Variety of Gifts

1. Madeleine L'Engle, *Walking on Water*, p. 18.

Chapter 18: Unless You Become...

1. *Directory for Masses with Children*, art. 21.
2. Ibid., art. 34.

Chapter 20: One Dancer's Vision

1. *CSL*, art. 30.
2. *DMC*, art. 33; *EACW*, art. 35.
3. *EACW*, arts. 35, 5.
4. Ibid., art. 56.
5. Ibid., art. 55.
6. Ibid., art. 59.
7. *CSL*, art. 17; *EACW* arts. 56, 34.
8. *CSL*, art. 19.
9. *EACW*, art. 26; see also *CSL*, arts. 122, 127.

Bibliography

Adams, Doug. *Congregational Dancing in Christian Worship.* Vallejo, Calif.: Enabling Company, 1972.

Backman, E. Louis. *Religious Dances in the Christian Church and in Popular Medicine.* Translated by E. Classen. Westport, Conn.: Greenwood Press, 1977; reprint of same title published in London: George Allen and Unwin, Ltd. 1952.

Deitering, Carolyn. *Actions, Gestures and Bodily Attitudes.* Saratoga, Calif.: Resource Publications, 1980.

_____. "Creative Movement Expression: Implications for the Liturgy." *Momentum* 2, no. 3 (October 1974): 18-23.

_____. "Filling Up on Emptiness." *Liturgy* 2, no. 1 (1981): 23-24.

_____. "The Graces of Age and Infirmity." *Liturgy* 2, no. 2 (1982): 19-23.

_____. "Movements for Young and Old Together." *Liturgy* 1, no. 3 (1981): 57-61.

_____. "A Space for Liturgical Action." *Liturgy* 3, no. 4 (1983): 42-45.

Fallon, Dennis and Wolbers, Mary Jane, ed. *Focus on Dance X: Religion and Dance.* Reston, Vir.: American Alliance for Health, Physical Education, Recreation and Dance, 1982.

Fisher, Constance. *Dancing the Old Testament.* Austin, Tex.: The Sharing Company, 1980.

_____. *Dancing With Early Christians.* The Sharing Company, 1983.

Huck, Gabe, ed. *The Liturgy Documents.* Chicago: The Liturgy Training Program, 1980.

Kirk, Martha Ann. *Dancing With Creation: Mexican and Native American Dance in Christian Worship and Education.* Saratoga, Calif.: Resource Publications, 1983.

de Lenval, Hélène Lubienska. *The Whole Man at Worship: The Actions of Man Before God.* London: Geoffrey Chapman, 1961.

van der Leeuw, Gerardus. *Sacred and Profane Beauty: The Holy in Art.* New York: Holt, Rinehart and Winston, 1963.

Mettler, Barbara. *Materials of Dance as a Creative Art Activity.* Tucson: Mettler Studios, 1979.

Moynahan, Michael, S.J. *Embodied Prayer.* Kansas City: NCR Publishing Company.

Oesterley, W.O.E. *The Sacred Dance.* Cambridge, England: At the University Press, 1923.

Parabola 4, no. 2, issue on theme of sacred dance (May 1979).

Sachs, Curt. *World History of the Dance.* New York: W.W. Norton and Company, 1937.

Searle, Mark. "Liturgical Gestures." *Assembly* 6, no. 3 (December 1979): 73-80.

Taylor, Margaret Fisk. *A Time to Dance.* Philadelphia: United Church Press, 1967.

Tucci, Douglass Shand. "The High Mass as Sacred Dance." *Theology Today* 34, no. 1 (April 1977): 58-72.

Wosien, Maria-Garbriele. *Sacred Dance: Encounter With the Gods.* New York: Avon Books, 1974.